Jesus, the Divine Physician

CHRISTOPH CARDINAL SCHÖNBORN

Jesus, the Divine Physician

Reflections on the Gospel during the Year of Luke

Translated by Henry Taylor

IGNATIUS PRESS SAN FRANCISCO

Original German edition:
Jesus, Arzt der Kranken: Gedanken zum Evangelium im Lukasjahr

Cover art:
This painting of the Crucifixion, which hangs in the diocesan administrative offices of the archbishop's palace in Vienna, was attacked and defaced by the Hitler Youth who stormed the palace on October 8, 1938.

Author's photograph:

ISBN 978-1-58617-180-3
Library of Congress Control Number 2007938140
Printed in the United States of America ∞

Contents

Lent and the Easter Season

Feasts in the Church Year

Introduction

A few years ago, within the framework of an ecumenical celebration and dedication, I was able to visit the new operational center of the Workers' Samaritan Association in Vienna.

The Workers' Samaritan Association (no connection with the British Samaritans) is a kind of local Red Cross with a clear commitment to social democracy. For a long time, Austrian Socialists were reputed to be—and many of them were—critical of the Church, or even opposed to her. That was part of the sad heritage of the division in our country [Austria] that led in 1934 to a brief but violent civil war. The tragic division of the country into "blacks" and "reds" played no small part in the illegal rise of the "browns", the National Socialists [Nazis], which ended with the *Anschluss*, the annexation of Austria [to Germany]. The picture of the crucifixion that hung in the archbishop's palace in Vienna (shown on the cover of this book) and that was vandalized by fanatical Hitler Youth members is a symbol of the way that only the common suffering under the Nazi persecution brought "reds" and "blacks" together again. Against this background, the dedication to which I just referred was moving and symbolic.

Why am I mentioning this in the introduction to the Gospel readings of the "year of Luke"? On account of the name Workers' Samaritan Association! The image of the good Samaritan comes from the Gospel. It is among the best known of Jesus' parables. It has become the standard example of loving one's neighbor, far beyond the circles of Church "insiders"—so much so, that a completely "red" organization sees its work in helping the victims of accidents, needy people, and the sick as "Samaritan work", without its having any connection with the Church. It is simply a matter of helping one's neighbor who is in need, irrespective of his race, religion, or political views.

The parable of the good Samaritan, however, is found only in Luke's Gospel. It is about Luke and his Gospel that we are now talking, and, in the following pages, that Gospel will be our guide through all the Sundays of the Church's year (Lectionary year C).

Each of the four Gospel writers has his own style, his own sources, his own emphases, and things that only he tells us about. Only all four together produce the whole and unmistakable picture of Jesus. Each of the Gospels adds its own particular note, so that we are quite right in talking about the picture of Christ in the Gospel of Matthew or the picture of Christ in the Gospel of John—and certainly also the picture of Christ in the Gospel of Luke.

It is only in the four canonical Gospels that the Church has recognized the canonical picture of Christ, the true and original picture. It is certainly not by chance that these are also the four oldest accounts of Jesus that we have. The many other gospels, which without exception are clearly later, were not recognized by the Church as being genuine, even if there may be one or another original saying of Jesus in them. Almost every year, one of these numerous so-called apocryphal gospels is brought forward as a new sensation, as happened just recently with the gospel of Judas. Usually it is not mentioned that people have known about them for a long time and that the works have been studied by specialists. Saint Irenaeus of Lyons, for instance, talks about the gospel of Judas at the end of the second century and demonstrates that it is a late forgery.

But what argues far more strongly in favor of the genuineness of the four oldest Gospels is their incomparable spiritual power. Jesus himself is speaking in them. His spirit, his heart, and his transforming power can be felt at work in them. They are not just human discourse and human wisdom. They are also that; but, shot through with the fire of the Holy Spirit, they are truly God's word.

What picture would we have of Jesus without the parable of the good Samaritan? How much, altogether, would be missing from our picture of Jesus if we had no Gospel of Luke! I myself was almost horrified when I discovered, with the help of a synopsis (that is, a parallel edition of the four Gospels), how much of what is quite essential in our picture of Jesus is owed to Luke's alertness in bringing it all together.

Only he tells us the three parables about the way that God's love patiently seeks for us men: the parable of the lost sheep, the parable of the lost penny, and above all—perhaps Jesus' best-known parable—the parable of the prodigal son (Lk 15). What a marvelous picture of God Jesus offers us in this parable!

Only Luke has passed on to us the disturbing parable of the gluttonous rich man and Lazarus (Lk 16:19–31). And the parable of the Pharisee who praises himself before God and the tax collector who is sorrowfully aware of his sins (Lk 18:9–14)—how it speaks to us! That, too, is found only in Luke.

Thanks to Luke, we know a great deal about the life and the suffering of Jesus, such as is presented in the precious and impressive story about the wealthy little man Zacchaeus, who was not ashamed to climb a tree in order to be able to see Jesus, even though Zacchaeus was a despised "bloodsucker" (Lk 19:1–10).

Thanks to Luke, we know some important things about Jesus' Passion. Only Luke tells us about Jesus sweating blood during his sorrow unto death, about his agony, and about the angel sent to strengthen him (Lk 22:43–44). Only Luke has preserved the deeply disturbing little scene in which Jesus, after Peter's betrayal, turns around and looks at him. "And [he] wept bitterly", it says about Peter. That is how it is for everyone who meets that gaze in his heart—that gaze, free of all accusation, which brings tears of repentance for the betrayal of love (Lk 22:61–62).

Only Luke refers to the way that Jesus forgives not only Peter, his disciple who betrayed him, but also those who crucified him: "Father, forgive them; for they know not what they do" (Lk 23:34).

Only Luke is able to tell us of the marvelous transformation brought about in the righteous thief by Jesus' loving forgiveness: "Jesus, remember me when you come in your kingly power"—"Today you will be with me in Paradise" (Lk 23:42–43).

All these examples from the material peculiar to Luke show that the author has emphasized in a particular way Jesus' turning toward sinners, as well as his love for the poor, the sick, and those who have lost their way. Luke did not invent all that; he discovered it. This is because Luke, who was a doctor by profession and whom Paul calls "beloved" (Col 4:14), undertook thorough researches for his Gospel and thereby obviously uncovered many sources (oral and perhaps also written) concerning Jesus. We can understand how for Luke, the doctor, Jesus' concern for every kind of suffering was especially important. It may also be connected with his calling as a doctor that Luke is such an accurate and reliable historian who went into everything carefully, so as to be able to talk about Jesus and his activity as reliably as possible.

Only Luke prefaced his Gospel with a foreword: "Inasmuch as many have undertaken to compile a narrative of the things which have been accomplished among us, just as they were delivered to us by those who from the beginning were eyewitnesses and ministers of the word, it seemed good to me also, having followed all things closely for some time past, to write an orderly account for you, most excellent Theophilus, that you may know the truth concerning the things of which you have been informed" (Lk 1:1–4).

Starting from the basics, from the first beginnings, Luke intends to look at all that has happened. What would we know about the beginnings without the Gospel of Luke? It is to him that we owe the first two chapters, about the conception and birth of John the Baptist and of Jesus himself, which lay the foundations for the story. The Gospel for Christmas is found in Luke, and only there, just as it is only through him that we know about the Presentation of Jesus in the temple, forty days after his birth, and about his visit to the temple at the age of twelve.

Where did Luke get his information about the beginning of Jesus' life on earth? An old tradition saw Luke as being very close to Mary, the Mother of our Lord. Who else but Mary could, in the end, be the source for reports about the Annunciation by the angel and about Jesus' being conceived by the Holy Spirit? Although in their literary form these accounts may well have been strongly influenced by examples from the Old Testament, nonetheless, the "infancy Gospel" of Saint Luke is essentially an account about real and miraculous events: things that really happened in history, "in the days of Herod" (Lk 1:5), in the days of Caesar Augustus (see Lk 2:1), just as Luke sets John's public ministry (see Lk 3:1–3) and that of Jesus himself within the framework of world history; and miraculous, since this account embodies God's sovereign activity in the world. Not in all-powerful Rome, whence the Emperor Augustus rules over all peoples, but in the manger in Bethlehem, there is born the one called "Son of the Most High" [Lk 1:32], and that indeed is who he is. The poet Virgil had sung of Rome, "imperium sine fine dedi" (I have given you a rule without end). Yet only of that child in Bethlehem is it indeed true, that "of his kingdom there will be no end" (Lk 1:33).

Thus it is only logical that Luke brings his second book, the "Gospel of Church history", the Acts of the Apostles, to an end in Rome, where Paul, as a prisoner, is spreading the teaching about Jesus "quite openly and unhindered" (Acts 28:31) in the power of the Spirit of Jesus. For the Apostles' task was to bear witness "to the end of the earth" (Acts 1:8), to what was at the beginning of the Good News: "To you is born this day in the city of David a Savior, who is Christ the Lord" (Lk 2:11).

Christ the Savior! That, quite simply, is the message of Saint Luke the doctor.

Let us return to the blessing of the Workers' Samaritan Association operational center that we mentioned at the beginning. At the close of the celebration, the manager of the center invited me into his office. He had an icon there, he said, and would I please bless that, too? He had had it painted specially. It represents the good Samaritan—an appropriate subject for this place. Yet the manager pointed out to me something particularly interesting about this icon. He explained to me that in the tradition of the Eastern Church, Christ himself is portrayed as the good Samaritan. The badly wounded man lying beside the highway is mankind, all of us. Christ did not pass us by in our hour of need. He bound up our wounds and brought us home to the Father's inn. This marvelous parable is talking about Christ himself. Anyone who takes the good Samaritan for his example is imitating Christ.

These few brief remarks, about this and that, certainly mention only a small part of what could be said about Luke. One really ought to make a special point of the central role played in his Gospel by the prayers of Jesus and those close to him. Every day, the Church throughout the world prays the three great prayers from the "infancy narratives": the *Benedictus* of Zechariah in the morning (Lk 1:68–79), Mary's *Magnificat* in the evening (Lk 1:46–55), and Simeon's *Nunc Dimittis* at night (Lk 2:29–32).

It is also important to mention the particular role of women in the Gospel of Luke, beginning with Mary, then Elizabeth and Anna, and then the women who accompany Jesus and give him financial support (Lk 8:1–3), right up to Mary and Martha, in whose home he found friends (Lk 10:38–42).

Many things barely mentioned here will have their say when it comes to the individual Gospel readings, however brief and concise. There is a lot else that deserves thinking about in every Gospel read on a Sunday.

Thus, there is one thing I dearly hope: may it be, for all those who read these commentaries on the Gospel readings, a little bit as it was for the disciples at Emmaus. That, too, is a story that only Luke tells. How thankful we should be that he has given it to us!

As they are walking, Jesus explains Holy Scripture to the two stunned disciples (who have not yet recognized him)—above all, he explains what has been written about him, the Messiah, Jesus Christ. They invite their unrecognized fellow traveler to be their guest, and when he comes in with them and they find how he prays and breaks the bread, then they recognize him, and they return with hearts afire to the others in Jerusalem (Lk 24:13–35).

My greatest reward will be if the brief expositions in this book, of parts of the Gospel of Luke, do a little to help as many people as possible to have the same experience as the disciples at Emmaus. I must again thank the *Kroner Zeitung* for this third volume, which completes a trilogy of commentaries on the Sunday Gospel readings from all three years of the liturgical lectionary, and also thank its legendary editor Hans Dichand. He has made it possible for me to publish most of the material here in his newspaper, *Sunday by Sunday*, in the year 2003–2004. My thanks to the team from the Krone Bunt, who patiently dealt with the layout of my text for the German edition. Thanks also to our team in publishing, who always copy out my handwritten texts (I can still not make up my mind to use a computer for this), illustrate them, and, where necessary, abbreviate them. Finally, I thank all those who have helped to make this book out of the articles. My thanks to them all for their excellent teamwork.

And now, lastly, the most important thing of all: Luke's words are God's word in human speech. It is worthwhile, and essential, first of all to read the words of his Gospel carefully, and to meditate on them. My explanations and my reflections on them are simply meant to help. The power of God is there in the Gospel. May it work powerfully!

Vienna, The Feast of the Transfiguration of Christ
August 6, 2006

ADVENT

AND

THE CHRISTMAS SEASON

First Sunday of Advent

The Gospel of Luke 21:25–28, 34–36

[At that time, Jesus said to his disciples,] "There will be signs in sun and moon and stars, and upon the earth distress of nations in perplexity at the roaring of the sea and the waves, men fainting with fear and with foreboding of what is coming on the world; for the powers of the heavens will be shaken. And then they will see the Son of man coming in a cloud with power and great glory. Now when these things begin to take place, look up and raise your heads, because your redemption is drawing near. . . .

"But take heed to yourselves lest your hearts be weighed down with dissipation and drunkenness and cares of this life, and that day come upon you suddenly like a snare; for it will come upon all who dwell upon the face of the whole earth. But watch at all times, praying that you may have strength to escape all these things that will take place, and to stand before the Son of man."

A Different Advent

The First Sunday in Advent: the first candle is burning on the Advent wreath. The Advent markets and the Christmas shopping began long ago, of course. They no longer wait patiently for dear old Advent. The great Christmas tree has already been standing in front of the Rathaus in Vienna for quite a while. In many places, the Christmas lights were hung out weeks ago. The refreshment stands did not wait for the First Sunday in Advent, either. And why should they? They don't really have anything to do with Advent.

Why should we wait at all, in our impatient age? Everything always has to be there at once, be available for us straightaway. Are we still capable of waiting for the right time? All kinds of crops, and fruits, and vegetables are supposed to be equally available at all times of the year. And thus the pleasure of waiting for things is lost.

Yet Advent has to do with waiting. Advent means "coming". It is preparing for a coming or, more accurately, for someone who is going to come. It is not waiting for the "Christmas man", that strange mixture of Santa Claus, Saint Nicholas, and Father Frost, who has been invented in order to push the Christ child into the background. Advent is preparing for the coming of the Christ child. The expectation of the coming days and weeks is directed toward the silent, holy night of his birth in the poor stall at Bethlehem, and that makes Advent such a lovely time. Many people experience the joy of Advent when they take part in a Rorate Mass early in the morning in our churches.

Then, of course, we see a quite different side of Advent, the one addressed by today's Gospel. It is not just a matter of remembering Jesus' birth, which is represented everywhere by the crib. This is also the time for consciously looking forward to the second coming of Christ "with power and great glory".

Jesus promised that he would come again and that that would be the end of time and of the world. Then we will all have to give an account for our lives. Before that, however, there will be terrifying signs. Jesus mentions wars, famines, and persecutions. There has been plenty of all that in the past [twentieth] century. Today he is talking about terrifying natural phenomena on earth and among the stars. We are always reading in the newspaper about enormous flares shooting out from the surface of the sun, on which our life here on earth is completely dependent.

What is our attitude to news like that, which comes to us almost daily through the media? Many people, says Jesus, will be "fainting with fear". Panic and horror cripple people and fill them with "distress and perplexity". Yet such impulses may also bring a blessing. When our own lives are shaken to their foundations, when everything is tottering and relationships break down, when our own world collapses, then something entirely new may happen.

Then someone may personally experience the saying of Jesus, "Look up and raise your heads, because your redemption is drawing near." Perhaps I had to pass through these catastrophes so that I could become aware and recognize that God is coming into my life. "If nothing happens, then nothing will happen." If my world is shaken, then God's world can open up for me. Then Advent is happening, not without pain, and yet with a joy that is all the greater.

Second Sunday of Advent

The Gospel of Luke 3:1–6

In the fifteenth year of the reign of Tiberius Caesar, Pontius Pilate being governor of Judea, and Herod being tetrarch of Galilee, and his brother Philip tetrarch of the region of Ituraea and Trachonitis, and Lysanias tetrarch of Abilene, in the high-priesthood of Annas and Caiaphas, the word of God came to John the son of Zechariah in the wilderness; and he went into all the region about the Jordan, preaching a baptism of repentance for the forgiveness of sins. As it is written in the book of the words of Isaiah the prophet,

"The voice of one crying in the wilderness:
Prepare the way of the Lord,
make his paths straight.
Every valley shall be filled,
and every mountain and hill shall be brought low,
and the crooked shall be made straight,
and the rough ways shall be made smooth;
and all flesh shall see the salvation of God."

Not Just Stories

Fairy stories usually begin something like this: "Once upon a time there was a king . . .", or, "A long, long time ago there lived with his wife a poor fisherman. . . ." There are no precise details as to date or time in a fairy story. Nor are we told where the action is happening. It happened sometime, somewhere. Time and place play no great part. It is a matter of typical human situations and fundamental experiences that are in some sense universally valid. Fairy stories tell a story, not history.

It is quite different with today's Gospel: it is reporting history; it is not telling stories. It talks about a particular moment in the history of the world, not about an indeterminate "long ago". It does not say, "Once upon a time . . ." but gives an exact date. The fifteenth year of the reign of the Emperor Tiberius was A.D. 27–28. At that time, the cruel Pontius Pilate was Roman governor of Judea; Herod the Great's two hated sons, both immoral and equally cruel, were local princes by the goodwill of the emperor. The two high priests are known to us from Jesus' trial.

At that time, then, things were not looking rosy and peaceful. These were bad times, just as, in fact, for most people most times are bad times, filled with affliction, poverty, and privation, and a hard struggle to survive. So at that time, exactly then, in the year 28–29, God intervened in this history, with its pain and suffering. How did that happen?

"The word of God came to John". God intervenes by calling people. And whenever people apprehend his call, God can work great things through them. So it was with someone such as Francis of Assisi (d. 1226) or Mother Teresa (d. 1997). They heard God's call and obeyed.

I am always asking myself, "How did those people hear God's call?" How did they know that it was not something they imagined, just self-deception? God does not call us up on the phone. How can his voice be distinguished from the babble of voices all around?

God's call went out to John "in the wilderness". In order for God to speak to me, I must hear him. In order to hear, I need a certain degree of quiet. That is why John was in the wilderness. The silence there is so complete that one's heart is quieted and starts to hear. In our world today, silence has become a rare commodity. That is why it is so important to me that our churches are open. Anyone looking for peace in the hectic everyday bustle will find it in the space in God's house, saturated as it is with prayer. Many people find that God speaks to their hearts there. They come to an inner clarity; they find consolation and help in decision making. If peace then comes into our own hearts, we can be sure that it comes from God.

But what did God say to John in the wilderness? Above all, these were words of hope. He was to prepare the way for the Lord—what was crooked should be made straight, and any difficulties be cleared away. God was to find room once more, and people were to be able to get to God. People like to portray John as the precursor. His story is not a fairy story. By the path that he prepared, God really did come to men: came as the little child at Bethlehem, as the Redeemer of all mankind. This true history began with Christmas.

THIRD SUNDAY OF ADVENT

The Gospel of Luke 3:10–18

And the multitudes asked [John], "What then shall we do?" And he answered them, "He who has two coats, let him share with him who has none; and he who has food, let him do likewise." Tax collectors also came to be baptized, and said to him, "Teacher, what shall we do?" And he said to them, "Collect no more than is appointed you." Soldiers also asked him, "And we, what shall we do?" And he said to them, "Rob no one by violence or by false accusation, and be content with your wages."

As the people were in expectation, and all men questioned in their hearts concerning John, whether perhaps he were the Christ, John answered them all, "I baptize you with water; but he who is mightier than I is coming, the thong of whose sandals I am not worthy to untie; he will baptize you with the Holy Spirit and with fire. His winnowing fork is in his hand, to clear his threshing floor, and to gather the wheat into his granary, but the chaff he will burn with unquenchable fire."

So, with many other exhortations, he preached good news to the people.

What to Do?

He was certainly no advocate of a "policy of appeasement", not a man for glossing things over and playing things down.

His preaching was anything but mild and gentle. What John the Baptist gave the multitude of people who came to him down by the Jordan took one's breath away. "You brood of vipers", he called them. They should not presume anything on account of being children of Abraham. "God is able from these stones to raise up children to Abraham." And to make clear to them how serious the situation was, he warned them, "Even now the axe is laid to the root of the trees; every tree therefore that does not bear good fruit is cut down and thrown into the fire" [Mt 3:7, 9–10].

John did not mince his words. He showed courage in not hesitating to criticize the great and the powerful. The prince who ruled Galilee, Herod (son of Herod the Great), had taken the wife of his brother Philip. John publicly criticized this marriage. Vengeance was not slow in coming. Herodias, the wife in question, used the first opportunity to have John beheaded.

Despite his brave words of criticism—or perhaps because of them—people came to John in droves and had themselves ducked in the Jordan by him as a sign of repentance and conversion.

Now comes the surprising thing: "What should we do?" asked his audience, in consternation. Strongly as he had preached repentance, his suggestions now were simple. What should we do to change our lives? No great steps, nothing impossible, no tremendous penitential practices—no, he did not demand that everyone should go into the wilderness like him to practice a strictly ascetic life there. Just make a start! Share what you have! You ought not to give everything away, but something . . . If you have more clothes than you really need, then give some to the person who has few clothes; and the same with food—share any surplus, if you have some; give someone else something to eat, too. Start by sharing. That is how children learn to fight against selfishness.

Customs officials, too, the feared and hated tax collectors, came for this baptism of repentance. "What should we do?" —"Collect no more than is appointed you." In other words, "Do your work. The state needs taxes. But beware of corruption, that scourge that distorts social relationships in so many countries. Do your work honestly and decently." In our country [Austria], we would have to add, "Do not exploit the welfare state to an unlimited extent! That destroys society."

The soldiers came, too: "What should we do?" "Do not do what *soldateska** so often do to this day: mistreat people, extort money from them, and plunder and torture them. Behave in proper fashion! Be the ones who protect the people, not the ones who exploit them."

That is how simple they are, the suggestions of the great preacher of repentance. What God expects of you is simply this: that you behave yourselves as decent human beings. Anything else leads to disaster. John was the precursor. He was trying to prepare people for Christ, the Messiah. Advent is the right time for that. Doing the simple things is not always simple, but it is certainly the best way to prepare for Christmas.

* *Soldateska* was a derogatory epithet used in the nineteenth and early twentieth centuries by labor movement activists who saw soldiers as thugs in the pay of capitalists.—Ed.

Fourth Sunday of Advent

The Gospel of Luke 1:39–45

In those days Mary arose and went with haste into the hill country, to a city of Judah, and she entered the house of Zechariah and greeted Elizabeth. And when Elizabeth heard the greeting of Mary, the child leaped in her womb; and Elizabeth was filled with the Holy Spirit and she exclaimed with a loud cry, "Blessed are you among women, and blessed is the fruit of your womb! And why is this granted me, that the mother of my Lord should come to me? For behold, when the voice of your greeting came to my ears, the child in my womb leaped for joy. And blessed is she who believed that there would be a fulfillment of what was spoken to her from the Lord."

Two Pregnant Women

An old tradition says that Saint Luke, the author of the third Gospel, was an artist. We know from the Apostle Paul, whom Luke accompanied on his missionary journeys, that Luke was a doctor by profession. That is why Luke is the patron saint of doctors. Whether he really was an artist, a painter, we do not know for sure. What is certain is that artists, too, have venerated Saint Luke as their heavenly patron for a long time. Many ancient icons, especially ones depicting Mary, are attributed to Saint Luke as an artist.

Legends usually have a core of truth. No Evangelist has

given us so many scenes from the life of Jesus that artists have found moving and inspiring. Thanks to him, we have the Gospel story of the birth of Jesus in Bethlehem. No other theme, apart from depictions of the crucifixion, has been used so often in art as the Christmas scene, with the newborn child in the crib. If we include plastic representations (especially crib scenes) as well as pictures, then these are innumerable.

Luke was a master at providing artistic themes. We will meet them again and again in the course of this year, which began on the First Sunday in Advent, for this is the year in which it is mostly parts of the Gospel of Luke that are read.

This Sunday's theme is picturesque and has been painted innumerable times by artists of every century. In earlier times it used to be called "the Visitation". It is Mary's visit to her relative, Elizabeth.

It was mostly the moment of meeting that caught the artist's eye. Mary is coming into Elizabeth's house and greeting her. That is the moment the artists have caught for us. The two pregnant women are greeting each other. Mary, the younger one, still just at the beginning of her pregnancy, is embracing Elizabeth, the older woman who had been sterile and who now, despite her age, has become pregnant by a miracle and is already in her sixth month.

Two pregnant women embrace each other. The subject moves our hearts, for each of these women carries beneath her heart a child, and that is always something mysterious. Each of us began our lives there, in our mother's womb. And every mother keeps her child in her heart, even long after the birth.

Yet Luke puts into words what cannot be portrayed pictorially. The children, too, greet each other. Elizabeth can feel how her child, John the Baptist, who will one day prepare the way for Jesus, leaps in her womb. His mother is aware of what is happening at this greeting—in fact, she puts it into words. She greets her young relative as "the mother of my Lord". Elizabeth is not just rejoicing that Mary has come to help her. She rejoices still more that Mary brings with her Jesus, the "blessed fruit of her womb".

In each Hail Mary, Elizabeth's greeting is repeated. The joy is always on account of Mary's bringing Jesus, that through her Jesus does not just come into "the house of Zechariah" but into every house. For Mary is still on her way to bring Jesus, her child, to people. That is what she means to do at Christmas, in every home.

Christmas Night

The Gospel of Luke 2:1–14

In those days a decree went out from Caesar Augustus that all the world should be enrolled. This was the first enrollment, when Quirinius was governor of Syria. And all went to be enrolled, each to his own city. And Joseph also went up from Galilee, from the city of Nazareth, to Judea, to the city of David, which is called Bethlehem, because he was of the house and lineage of David, to be enrolled with Mary his betrothed, who was with child.

And while they were there, the time came for her to be delivered. And she gave birth to her first-born son and wrapped him in swaddling cloths, and laid him in a manger, because there was no place for them in the inn.

And in that region there were shepherds out in the field, keeping watch over their flock by night. And an angel of the Lord appeared to them, and the glory of the Lord shone around them, and they were filled with fear. And the angel said to them, "Be not afraid; for behold, I bring you good news of a great joy which will come to all the people; for to you is born this day in the city of David a Savior, who is Christ the Lord. And this will be a sign for you: you will find a baby wrapped in swaddling cloths and lying in a manger." And suddenly there was with the angel a multitude of the heavenly host praising God and saying,

"Glory to God in the highest,
and on earth peace among men with whom he is pleased!"

"Bethlehem is a sad town", the Catholic mayor, Hanna Nasser, said a little while ago. Things have not substantially improved since then. The city of Jesus' birth has long been, and still is, powerless, entangled in the bloody conflict between Israel and the Palestinians.

He whose birth we are celebrating at Christmas was also powerless. It was someone else who had the power: the Emperor Augustus, the ruler of the greatest empire in the world at that time. The Roman empire, like all the empires of this world, needed a great deal of money, above all for its powerful military machine. For those purposes it required gigantic resources in terms of taxes, and the emperor had to know where he could get those taxes. That is why he had tax rolls drawn up throughout the whole empire, even in Israel, which was under Roman rule.

Many of the Jewish people refused to pay taxes to the emperor. They joined various liberation movements, which carried on either passive or active resistance to the authorities of occupation—and, indeed, which were not afraid of engaging in terrorist activity. These enthusiasts, who were called "zealots", repeatedly attempted to shake off the yoke of the occupying power. The Romans took cruel revenge, and many of the zealots ended up on the cross.

Joseph was not one of them; he obeyed the emperor's orders and, without much comment, did what had to be done. Even though his wife was in the later stages of pregnancy, he undertook, along with her, the wearisome journey—on foot or on a donkey—to Bethlehem, the city from which King David came, "because he was of the house and lineage of David".

Joseph, a poor man though from a royal family, had to submit to the emperor's rule. Yet the emperor, for his part, was subject to God's rule. Only God is almighty, and the emperor has only a delegated power. His life, like any man's, is in God's hand.

Thus it is God himself who arranged that Joseph had to travel to Bethlehem, the city of David, on account of the emperor's command. According to God's plan, the child that Mary was expecting had to be born in that city, from which the prophets said that one day the Messiah would come.

The powerful emperor was acting so as to serve God's plans—that is what Luke the Evangelist is telling us, and he was particularly sensitive to the arrangements God made. But what a contrast! The two travelers cannot find anyone to take them in; there is no room for the young woman in advanced pregnancy. In his hometown of Bethlehem, Joseph cannot find a roof over his head, although he is an offspring of David.

A manger and swaddling cloths are shelter for the child who is born. Extreme poverty and powerlessness: thus he came into this world, he who is the real Lord of the world and of history.

Why did God choose this way—why not a way of coming that everyone could see, one that everyone would hear about? I think there were two reasons, above all: First, to speak to our hearts. A little child moves almost any human being. God does not want to dominate us; he wants the love of our hearts. That is why he stretches out to us the arms of a child. Second, however, he does not want us to encounter one another threateningly, striking attitudes of power, but serving one another. If God makes himself so small in Christ, then we should not be making ourselves out to be great.

Bethlehem is everywhere. Sorrow, violence, and injustice

are dominant throughout the world. Where is there hope? Is there "a great joy"? Are angels proclaiming peace upon earth? Anyone who bends down to the child in the crib will find peace and joy.

Feast of the Holy Family

The Gospel of Luke 2:41–52

Now [Jesus'] parents went to Jerusalem every year at the feast of the Passover. And when he was twelve years old, they went up according to custom; and when the feast was ended, as they were returning, the boy Jesus stayed behind in Jerusalem. His parents did not know it, but supposing him to be in the company they went a day's journey, and they sought him among their kinsfolk and acquaintances; and when they did not find him, they returned to Jerusalem, seeking him. After three days they found him in the temple, sitting among the teachers, listening to them and asking them questions; and all who heard him were amazed at his understanding and his answers. And when they saw him they were astonished; and his mother said to him, "Son, why have you treated us so? Behold, your father and I have been looking for you anxiously." And he said to them, "How is it that you sought me? Did you not know that I must be in my Father's house?" And they did not understand the saying which he spoke to them. And he went down with them and came to Nazareth, and was obedient to them; and his mother kept all these things in her heart.

And Jesus increased in wisdom and in stature, and in favor with God and man.

Father, mother, and child—a family, a small family. They enjoy the happiness of being together. They are poor, even though the father is descended from the ancient royal race of David. They live in Nazareth. He is an artisan, a carpenter by trade. A few relatives are known to us by name. Otherwise, nothing is known about them.

And yet one thing is said: Joseph, the husband, is said to have been "just" [Mt 1:19], an honest, upright man. And something else: there was a secret between him and her, between Joseph and Mary. While she was still betrothed, she had become pregnant—but not by him. He had not wanted to make any scandal. He had simply been thinking about separating from her quite quietly, without exposing her, until he was let into the secret: the Father of this child is not another man—it is God who has made this gift. He believed, and trusted her, and gave God credit for something that is humanly incomprehensible.

It was in Bethlehem that he came into the world, this child who was God's gift. There had been special signs on the night of his birth: shepherds, telling a tale of angels, came to look at the child. Wise men came specially from the East, guided by signs in the stars, to worship this child as king. In the temple at Jerusalem, an old man uttered mysterious prophecies over the child when the child's parents dedicated him to God, in accordance with Jewish custom, forty days after his birth. Then something dramatic happened—next there was the hurried flight into Egypt, and finally the return home to Nazareth. What would become of this child, for whom such great things had been predicted? How often that question must have concerned his parents!

Now came something really surprising: nothing at all happened, nothing except the quite ordinary everyday life of the family of a poor artisan; day by day, there was work, worrying about orders, the efforts to earn what was needed. We hear nothing about miracles or extraordinary occurrences. This is an unprepossessing, hidden life in an insignificant little village. Only one thing gave this life a special radiance: love reigned among the three of them, and God was given first place, with the Jewish daily prayers, the visit to the synagogue on the sabbath, and the usual pilgrimage to Jerusalem each year at the Passover.

And so it went on, for thirty long years. The question that interests me is, what was everyday life at Nazareth like? What did they talk about, Joseph, Mary, and Jesus? Work? The troubles of their relatives? The political situation? Their faith? God's ways and his plans? We know none of that, and the Bible is simply silent about it all. That silence tells us that God is to be found in everyday life, in our little everyday cares, in our daily efforts to achieve kindness, patience, and honesty. If Jesus is God, who has lived as a man among us, then I can find him in everyday life, in the midst of my ordinary life.

Just once in those long years, we catch a glimpse of the mystery of Jesus, when he stayed behind in Jerusalem without telling his parents. We can sympathize with the anxiety of his parents and the way they felt hurt, and likewise with their reproachful tone when they finally found him after three anxious days. His answer must have hurt them:

"Why is it that you sought me? After all, I have to be about my Father's business." That was a painful insight: "This child does not belong to us. He comes from God; God is his Father." Mary did not argue; she kept all that in her heart, took it in as part of her life at Nazareth for all the years to come. She was truly living with God in everyday life.

New Year's Day
(Mary, Mother of God)

The Gospel of Luke 2:16–21

And [the shepherds] went with haste, and found Mary and Joseph, and the baby lying in a manger. And when they saw it they made known the saying which had been told them concerning this child; and all who heard it wondered at what the shepherds told them. But Mary kept all these things, pondering them in her heart. And the shepherds returned, glorifying and praising God for all they had heard and seen, as it had been told them.

And at the end of eight days, when he was circumcised, he was called Jesus, the name given by the angel before he was conceived in the womb.

Jesus and Mary

Eight days have passed since Christmas. All the commotion of New Year's Day has banished the silence of the holy night. In turbulent times, it is a help to find space for being reflective. Today's Gospel reading invites us to do just that.

Once again we see the shepherds, who came from the open field near Bethlehem and found that what the angel, God's messenger, had said was confirmed. They recounted it, and other people repeated the tale. For a little while, it was the big news in the neighborhood: this newborn child is something special. People are promising a great future for him. He is supposed to set his people free, as the great King David did centuries ago. Thus people are talking about him and puzzling over it all, and hopes arise—but probably doubts as well: How is this child of poor parents supposed to become a savior for the whole people?

While people are talking, and then probably soon moving on to the next subject of local news, Mary takes a different attitude. Is it not the case with most people, that they take to heart everything to do with their child, that they keep it in their heart and ponder it? A mother misses nothing, none of her child's smiles, not a word that is said about him. And her heart is moved by many impressions, hopes, and fears: What is going to become of my child?

Mary did not just have vague impressions to go on. She had not been given her child by Joseph. God had made her a gift of the child, after she had given the angel her assent to God's plan. Other people might doubt whether it was so, might cast suspicion on her, might say she had "slipped up". She knew whence this child that she had received had come. She kept in her memory every word the angel had said to her about her child's future. Why should I not believe her? Joseph, her fiancé, believed her.

It does me good to gaze on Mary at the beginning of a new year and to see how she deals with her personal story. Her attitude would do us good: keeping quiet and pondering how God is doing things in my life; looking at wherever he gives me a sign that he is laying down the central theme of my life's path. I think we will be astonished to see, once we are "on the other side", how everything works together and has its significance.

Today, eight days after Christmas, there is a twofold rite in accordance with Jewish custom: name giving and circumcision. Thus Jesus is identified as a Jew. Circumcision is the external sign of belonging to the people with whom God made his covenant. You cannot separate Jesus from his people, even though he is the subject of controversy among Jews to this day.

His name, too, shows unambiguously that he is a Jew: "Yeshua", or "Jesus", was a common name in those days. It expresses a great hope, for it means "God saves". And that is how the angel explains to Joseph the name that he is to give the child whom Mary has conceived: "He will save his people from their sins" [Mt 1:21]. We Christians believe that this name has another, deeper meaning: "Jesus" means not only that God is the Savior but that Jesus himself is the God who saves, who became a human child in order to make us children of God. At the beginning of the year, we find two names that can be our guide through all the days to come: Jesus and Mary.

Second Sunday after Christmas Day

The Gospel of John 1:1–18

In the beginning was the Word, and the Word was with God, and the Word was God. He was in the beginning with God; all things were made through him, and without him was not anything made that was made. In him was life, and the life was the light of men. The light shines in the darkness, and the darkness has not overcome it.

There was a man sent from God, whose name was John. He came for testimony, to bear witness to the light, that all might believe through him. He was not the light, but came to bear witness to the light.

The true light that enlightens every man was coming into the world. He was in the world, and the world was made through him, yet the world knew him not. He came to his own home, and his own people received him not. But to all who received him, who believed in his name, he gave power to become children of God; who were born, not of blood nor of the will of the flesh nor of the will of man, but of God.

And the Word became flesh and dwelt among us, full of grace and truth; we have beheld his glory, glory as of the only-begotten Son from the Father. (John bore witness to him, and cried, "This was he of whom I said, 'He who comes after me ranks before me, for he was before me.' ") And from his fulness have we all received, grace upon grace. For the law was given through Moses; grace and truth came through Jesus Christ. No one has ever seen God; the only-begotten Son, who is in the bosom of the Father, he has made him known.

In the Beginning

What was in the beginning, when everything began? The Big Bang, so many scientists say nowadays. Everything started with that, they say. Decisive things took place in the first few seconds and minutes, and the course had been set for the further development of the universe. Thus stars could appear, stars in inconceivable multitudes, and could group themselves into galaxies. One of these is our own Milky Way, in which our sun is circling together with its planets—one of which is our earth. Life has come into existence on earth, and finally man.

This, immensely oversimplified, is how science today sees the beginning and what came from it.

"In the beginning God created the heavens and the earth." That is how the Bible starts (Gen 1:1). All those things that have come into existence do not take their origin from blind chance. And if everything really did begin with the Big Bang, then this means only that that is the way God created the world. The world did not come into being, and order did not establish itself, of its own accord. I cannot believe that everything sorted itself out by itself. Everything is so marvelously organized and interrelated that I find it far easier to believe that God created everything than to assume that it all fell into place like that by chance.

"In the beginning was the Word". That is how Jesus' beloved disciple, John, begins his Gospel. Before any beginning, before ever the world came into existence, the Word was already with God—indeed, it was, and is, itself God. It is not the Big Bang that is the beginning but the Word. Alternatively, we may translate it, "In the beginning was meaning."

"All things were made through him", John continues. Everything has meaning; nothing came into being in a meaningless fashion. I am surprised at how many people are able to believe that everything is to be ascribed to chance. Science actually demonstrates the exact opposite. It is constantly attempting to unravel everything and to understand it: atoms, molecules, genes, cells, and organisms. The whole of nature is like a great book written in a script that we have not yet completely deciphered. Yet one thing I am sure of: someone wrote this book. And the more we learn how to read it, the more we are astounded at how marvelous, how sublime, the text is that we are learning to read.

God wrote this book with his Word, and he gave the light of reason to us men, so that we may understand what he has to say to us through nature, through creation.

Yet John, the disciple of Jesus, also knows that there is a battle between light and darkness raging in men's hearts. We often act in a way contrary to all reason and do not follow the light of our conscience but allow ourselves to be dragged into doing evil.

That is why "the true light . . . was coming into the world". That is why "the Word became flesh and dwelt among us". Here John is speaking in solemn and mysterious terms. His words are like a hymn, a solemn chant. The event that was celebrated not long ago, the birth of a child in Bethlehem, is illuminated in its profundity by John. This child is not only a little newborn human; he is God's own Word, God's Son, who has come to us men. This child is the key to God's mysterious book. If you want to read the book of creation, if you want to understand what God is saying in the universe, in nature, in life, in man, then bow down over the crib. The child will disclose it to you: God made everything out of love, and he made it in love; and only love can comprehend the word, the meaning, that God has put into everything.

The Epiphany of the Lord

The Gospel of Matthew 2:1–12

Now when Jesus was born in Bethlehem of Judea in the days of Herod the king, behold, Wise Men from the East came to Jerusalem, saying, "Where is he who has been born king of the Jews? For we have seen his star in the East, and have come to worship him." When Herod the king heard this, he was troubled, and all Jerusalem with him; and assembling all the chief priests and scribes of the people, he inquired of them where the Christ was to be born. They told him, "In Bethlehem of Judea; for so it is written by the prophet:

'And you, O Bethlehem, in the land of Judah,
are by no means least among the rulers of Judah;
for from you shall come a ruler
who will govern my people Israel.' "

Then Herod summoned the Wise Men secretly and ascertained from them what time the star appeared; and he sent them to Bethlehem, saying, "Go and search diligently for the child, and when you have found him bring me word, that I too may come and worship him." When they had heard the king they went their way; and behold, the star which they had seen in the East went before them, till it came to rest over the place where the child was. When they saw the star, they rejoiced exceedingly with great joy; and going into the house they saw the child with Mary his mother, and they fell down and worshiped him. Then, opening their treasures, they offered him gifts, gold and frankincense and myrrh. And being warned in a dream not to return to Herod, they departed to their own country by another way.

Do the Stars Tell Us?

Is it there in the stars, what is awaiting us in the new year? Horoscopes are highly fashionable. Today, the astrologers make their official entrance. These men from the East—probably from Persia—lovingly referred to as "the Three Kings" in popular tradition, are called *magoi*—that is, "magicians"—in today's Gospel reading. The translation of the Bible in German offers us a word of explanation when it talks about "astrologers from the East".

Is astrology permissible, then? The Wise Men from the orient saw a particular "star" rising "in the East". The Wise Men probably belonged to those learned circles in Persia which at that period had an incredibly detailed and accurate knowledge of the movements of the stars. An eminent Austrian astronomer with a typical old Austrian name, Conradin Ferrari d'Ochieppo, devoted many years of his life to researching ancient astronomy, and, on that basis, he pointed out a particular conjunction of Jupiter and Saturn in the year 7 B.C., probably the "genuine" year of Christ's birth.

Do the stars and their conjunctions tell us something about our future? These astrologers thought so. For them, the star they saw in its ascension was a heavenly indicator of something important happening in the world. The birth of a "king of the Jews" was what they read in the stars. They have a feeling that a turning point in the history of the world has arrived.

But now the decisive point: gazing at the stars is not enough. It is a matter of setting out to travel yourself. The Wise Men from the East venture on a long journey. They are looking for the newborn king, that they "may . . . worship him". They are prepared to be guided in their search. In Jerusalem, they come upon the message of the prophets of old: the one they are seeking is to be born in Bethlehem. God's word helps them on their way. They let it point out the way for them. They are not deterred by being sent to this miserable little town of Bethlehem.

And there the star once more gives them light. Is this simply a star in the sky? Does it not already draw them toward a different light, which is radiating from the place to which they are traveling? Soon they will be finding the house, the child, and Mary his mother. The Wise Men kneel before the child Jesus and offer him the treasures they have brought. On their way home, they are no longer guided by a star but by a dream, which they obey.

Is it there in the stars, where our own path will lead? Even the stars may give me general guidance—they are, after all, God's creatures. Yet the future does not lie in the stars but in the hand of their Creator. He speaks to us in many different ways: through the inner voice of conscience; through his word in the Bible; through events, whether joyous or painful; and also through nature and its laws. God is speaking to us in all that. Yet we must set out ourselves to seek the way, to take the trouble to find it and our goal. How great is our joy, though, when we find in Jesus the one who is the true Morning Star, the Light of the world!

The Baptism of the Lord

The Gospel of Luke 3:15–16, 21–22

As the people were in expectation, and all men questioned in their hearts concerning John, whether perhaps he were the Christ, John answered them all, "I baptize you with water; but he who is mightier than I is coming, the thong of whose sandals I am not worthy to untie; he will baptize you with the Holy Spirit and with fire. . . .

Now when all the people were baptized, and when Jesus also had been baptized and was praying, the heaven was opened, and the Holy Spirit descended upon him in bodily form, as a dove, and a voice came from heaven, "You are my beloved Son; with you I am well pleased."

Coming Up Again like New

What moved Jesus to go down to John the Baptist on the Jordan and have himself baptized by him? What was baptism for, anyway? Why did Jesus take this ritual over, so that it has remained to this day something typical of Christians? And, finally, what does baptism mean today, two thousand years later? What prompts all these questions is today's feast, the Baptism of the Lord, which concludes the Christmas season.

There are lustrations, ritual baths, purification rites, in many religions. The sacred bathing in the Ganges in India; the so-called *mikvah*, the ritual bath in Judaism; the lustrations in Islam; baptism in Christianity: they all have to do with the way that bodily cleansing is also a symbol for freshening the soul, for spiritual renewal. Anyone who is able to take a good shower after he has finished work and is perhaps dirty and perspiring will find how refreshing that can be.

John had in mind a quite particular aim. His baptism was to prepare the way for someone. He knew in his heart that someone was to come after him who was greater than he was: the Messiah, the One who would set the people free. John merely intended to prepare people for the Messiah's coming. That is why he was stirring people up. His preaching was no "spring breeze"—it shook people, it spoke to their consciences, it demanded that they change their lives. And many people were moved to "convert", to turn their lives around, and came to him for baptism. He poured water from the Jordan over them as a sign of repentance and of purification.

Suddenly, Jesus was there, too, in the midst of the others who were crowding to be baptized by John. What was he doing there? Was he doing penance? Was he wanting to confess his sins? Was he wanting to be purified from his sins? If there was one person who did not need that, it was Jesus. What moved him to leave his hometown of Nazareth and to receive this baptism of repentance like one of all the other sinful men?

Right at the start of his public ministry, Jesus gives a sign. By doing so, he allows us to understand why he has given up the quiet and security of a carpenter's life. He shows us the significance of the new path he has taken: he is going about in the midst of people. He lines up along with the great crowd of sinners, as if he were one of them. His intention is to become one of us, yet not so as to become a miserable sinner like we are. For our sake, he is becoming one of us. He intends to carry our burdens and our sins—my burdens, and my sins. He takes them upon himself and carries them into the Jordan, to wash them away. He does not despise the people among whom he is taking his place. Later, he would say that he had not come to judge but to save.

God reaffirms this path: God's Spirit comes down upon him like a dove. A voice can be heard: "You are my beloved Son; with you I am well pleased." The path of Jesus that God attests goes downward to us men, down among us sinners. God is well pleased with this. That is what Jesus came for.

Yet the aim is not to remain down below. We come up again refreshed, from a bath. The person who was laden down with sins emerges from baptism like one newly created. The aim of baptism is to come up again renewed, like this. Jesus came down into the water of baptism with us, so as to draw us up out of our old burdens and sins, with him. That is the meaning of baptism to this day. We can renew it every day.

Sundays

in

Ordinary Time

Second Sunday in Ordinary Time

The Gospel of John 2:1–11

On the third day there was a marriage at Cana in Galilee, and the mother of Jesus was there; Jesus also was invited to the marriage, with his disciples. When the wine failed, the mother of Jesus said to him, "They have no wine." And Jesus said to her, "O woman, what have you to do with me? My hour has not yet come." His mother said to the servants, "Do whatever he tells you." Now six stone jars were standing there, for the Jewish rites of purification, each holding twenty or thirty gallons. Jesus said to them, "Fill the jars with water." And they filled them up to the brim. He said to them, "Now draw some out, and take it to the steward of the feast." So they took it. When the steward of the feast tasted the water now become wine, and did not know where it came from (though the servants who had drawn the water knew), the steward of the feast called the bridegroom and said to him, "Every man serves the good wine first; and when men have drunk freely, then the poor wine; but you have kept the good wine until now." This, the first of his signs, Jesus did at Cana in Galilee, and manifested his glory; and his disciples believed in him.

Do Whatever He Tells You

It began at a wedding. Jesus had just begun his public ministry. His name was not yet well known. His healings of the sick, which made him famous far and wide, he had not yet begun. Only a small group of disciples had gathered around him—among them John, who is responsible for reporting today's story.

So, a wedding was taking place in a village near Nazareth; then, as is still the case today in the troubled and strife-torn Middle East, it was a great feast with many guests. Among them was Mary of Nazareth, the Mother of Jesus. Her Son and his friends had been invited along with her. We still have a great deal to learn from Eastern hospitality.

We know nothing about the happy couple. They may well have been poor people, otherwise the wine would not have run out so soon. Being unable to offer anything to one's guests is deeply shameful. Mary grasped the unfortunate situation. She is on the lookout for every difficulty. That is why, to this day, so many people throughout the world come to Mary and confidently ask for her help.

What does she want from Jesus? She makes no demands; she does not lay down what he should do. She simply points out to him the uncomfortable position in which their hosts find themselves—nothing more. Her self-restraint is marvelous. She certainly could have put pressure on him: "Do something to help these people!" She did nothing of the sort—Mary respects her Son's freedom. She sets us a great example here.

Jesus' reaction seems rather brusque: "O woman, what have you to do with me?" That sounds far from friendly. He doesn't call her "Mother" but "woman"—almost as if she were a stranger. Is this the defensive reaction—so common—of not wanting to be "mothered"? Is Jesus clearly marking his distance from her, now that he has left the parental home to set out on the path he feels called to follow? This is certainly not an easy moment for Mary, getting an answer like that!

Yet Jesus has his reasons for refusing his Mother's request: "My hour has not yet come." It is not yet time for him to manifest himself through wonders and signs. Indeed, he probably did not see his mission as being primarily that at all. He does not want people to run after him on account of healings and miracles. He wants us to repent, to change our ideas, to turn our lives around. He is looking for faith, not admiration.

But Mary does not allow herself to be dissuaded. She keeps insisting that the bridal couple must be helped in their difficulty. And so she is confident that Jesus will certainly do it. "Do whatever he tells you", she says to the servants. And Jesus lets himself be moved by this confiding trust. He changes 120 gallons of water into exquisite wine—more than enough for a large wedding feast.

What is Jesus trying to tell us with this first miracle? First, that he rejoices in rejoicing—otherwise, he would not have come to the wedding feast; and second, that even quite ordinary material concerns move his heart. He does not always solve our difficulties quite as beautifully as he did at the wedding in Cana. Yet he can always work the miracle of transformation whenever he transforms the water of our everyday life, by faith, into the wine of joy and hope. Only, we do have to play our part—following Mary's advice, doing what she asks: Do what he tells you!

Third Sunday in Ordinary Time

The Gospel of Luke 1:1–4; 4:14–21

Inasmuch as many have undertaken to compile a narrative of the things which have been accomplished among us, just as they were delivered to us by those who from the beginning were eyewitnesses and ministers of the word, it seemed good to me also, having followed all things closely for some time past, to write an orderly account for you, most excellent Theophilus, that you may know the truth concerning the things of which you have been informed. . . .

And Jesus returned in the power of the Spirit into Galilee, and a report concerning him went out through all the surrounding country. And he taught in their synagogues, being glorified by all.

And he came to Nazareth, where he had been brought up; and he went to the synagogue, as was his custom, on the sabbath day. And he stood up to read; and there was given to him the book of the prophet Isaiah. He opened the book and found the place where it was written,

"The Spirit of the Lord is upon me,
because he has anointed me to preach good news to the poor.
He has sent me to proclaim release to the captives
and recovering of sight to the blind,
to set at liberty those who are oppressed,
to proclaim the acceptable year of the Lord."

And he closed the book, and gave it back to the attendant, and sat down; and the eyes of all in the synagogue were fixed on him. And he began to say to them, "Today this Scripture has been fulfilled in your hearing."

A Reliable Account

Regularly, as we get close to Christmas and Easter, quite a number of magazines and newspapers think they have to serve up sensational stories about Jesus. There is nothing to it all: we are told that Jesus did not die on the Cross at all but only appeared to be dead, or that he traveled off to India and finally died there as a guru; or secret writings found in the desert sands (writings that have long been known to scholars) are brought forward and are puffed up as great new discoveries about Jesus. The media want to reveal to us who this Jesus really was. They then like to present the picture of Jesus drawn by the Gospels as being distorted by piety, and they suggest that this piety has to be stripped away in order to uncover the genuine Jesus, unadulterated.

What is disappointing about these revelations is that the Jesus who emerges is mostly quite astoundingly close to whatever is the current fashion. In the days of my youth, it was the revolutionary "Che Guevara Jesus"; nowadays, he is usually a gentle esoteric teacher. That kind of picture of a fashionable Jesus already existed in early Christianity. We can find these depictions in the so-called apocrypha—those writings about Jesus that were rejected by the Church as being not genuine, as being later forgeries.

The Church maintained only four texts as genuine Gospels: Matthew, Mark, Luke, and John. It is not by chance that these are older than the apocryphal "gospels", which come, one and all, only from the second and third centuries.

Today we read the little foreword with which Luke the Evangelist prefaced his book. This is a precious testimony to the reliability of the reports in the Gospels. Let us not forget: right from the beginning, Jesus' followers took an interest in keeping an exact memory of his words and deeds and in passing on an equally exact account. These were of course the words and deeds of their revered and beloved Master. The people in the first Christian communities did not want to hear fairy stories or legends but careful and accurate reports. They wanted to know how it had been, what he had said and taught, what his dreadful suffering in Jerusalem had been like, and the wonderful thing that happened then, when he did not remain in the tomb but rose again.

Accounts like that were mainly by word of mouth. At that time, people still had extraordinary memories. They could repeat exactly, word for word, what they had heard from Jesus. So, in particular, people asked questions of the eyewitnesses of Jesus' life—those who had been with him on the road from the beginning. Two of the Evangelists were among their number: Matthew and John. Mark, as a youth, certainly knew Jesus, but Luke came along only later. We meet Luke as the Apostle Paul's companion, who went through many stages of Paul's travels with him and depicted them most vividly in his Acts of the Apostles.

Luke quite consciously intended to provide an account of Jesus that was reliable, the fruit of exact historical research, based on the original sources. Theophilus, to whom he dedicates his work, should know that his faith in Jesus has firm foundations. Reading Luke's Gospel some two thousand years later, we likewise should be able to rely not on having any fables or fairy stories put before us here but on what really happened at the time. Like Theophilus in the first century, the people of the twenty-first century can stake their lives on the Jesus we meet in the Gospels, and on his teaching.

Fourth Sunday in Ordinary Time

The Gospel of Luke 4:21–30

[Then in the synagogue, Jesus] began to say to them, "Today this Scripture has been fulfilled in your hearing." And all spoke well of him, and wondered at the gracious words which proceeded out of his mouth; and they said, "Is not this Joseph's son?" And he said to them, "Doubtless you will quote to me the proverb, 'Physician, heal yourself; what we have heard you did at Capernaum, do here also in your own country.' " And he said, "Truly, I say to you, no prophet is acceptable in his own country. But in truth, I tell you, there were many widows in Israel in the days of Elijah, when the heaven was shut up three years and six months, when there came a great famine over all the land; and Elijah was sent to none of them but only to Zarephath, in the land of Sidon, to a woman who was a widow. And there were many lepers in Israel in the time of the prophet Elisha; and none of them was cleansed, but only Naaman the Syrian." When they heard this, all in the synagogue were filled with wrath. And they rose up and put him out of the city, and led him to the brow of the hill on which their city was built, that they might throw him down headlong. But passing through the midst of them he went away.

Stay with Us!

Everyone knew him, back home in Nazareth. He had indeed come into the world in Bethlehem, but his home was in Nazareth. There he had grown up; there he had lived for thirty years; that was where his family lived. How these years—almost thirty—passed, we do not know. If there had been anything remarkable, we should certainly have been told about it. It had probably been a simple, everyday kind of life. Hardly anyone apart from Mary and Joseph probably knew anything about his secret.

But then, suddenly, came a break in the course of his life. He left home and began to preach in public. When he did so, miracles and healings occurred, and people were soon talking about him everywhere—even back home. No wonder that the whole village was really keen to see him again. Last Sunday we heard how, in accordance with his established custom, he went into the place of prayer, the synagogue, of his hometown on the sabbath. He was asked to give a reading from the Bible. The passage of Scripture that was due to be read talks about the promised Messiah, the hope of the Jewish people. When the Messiah comes, so the prophet promises, he will bring good news, a joyful message: the blind will see, the prisoners will be set free, and those broken by life will be healed.

When, astoundingly, Jesus declared, "Today this Scripture has been fulfilled in your hearing", then at first there was great enthusiasm. The expectations were still greater: "Now do here the things that we have heard that you have done elsewhere! You must especially perform striking signs and miracles here, in your hometown." The people in the town from which Jesus came were expecting a kind of special treatment from him. They felt it was his duty to pay them special attention since they all knew him, and they based their claim for miracles on that.

Did Jesus mean to provoke them? They have hardly voiced their wishes when Jesus rejects them absolutely: "No prophet is acceptable in his own country." In other words, "I shall not demonstrate my miraculous works for you but for the pagans. You think you know me because I grew up along with you. The pagans will believe in me, and that is why they will see miracles."

It is no wonder that the mood is completely reversed. The man they admired at first is the one they now want to kill. It is shocking how fickle people are. Perhaps we can recognize ourselves a little (or even quite clearly) in the people of Nazareth. How quickly it often comes about that enthusiasm reverses to become enmity or that togetherness reverses to become exclusiveness.

Jesus walks through the midst of the moving crowd, and no one dares to touch him. He leaves his hometown forever. Other people will give him a better welcome. Elsewhere he will find faith and be able to work effectively. Sometimes I am frightened by the notion that "Nazareth" might be here among us. We, with whom Jesus was "at home" for centuries, might drive him out from our midst with our unbelief. Then there comes to me the prayer, "Lord, do not leave us. We need you. Please stay with us!"

Fifth Sunday in Ordinary Time

The Gospel of Luke 5:1–11

While the people pressed upon him to hear the word of God, [Jesus] was standing by the lake of Gennesaret. And he saw two boats by the lake; but the fishermen had gone out of them and were washing their nets. Getting into one of the boats, which was Simon's, he asked him to put out a little from the land. And he sat down and taught the people from the boat. And when he had ceased speaking, he said to Simon, "Put out into the deep and let down your nets for a catch." And Simon answered, "Master, we toiled all night and took nothing! But at your word I will let down the nets." And when they had done this, they enclosed a great shoal of fish; and as their nets were breaking, they beckoned to their partners in the other boat to come and help them. And they came and filled both the boats, so that they began to sink. But when Simon Peter saw it, he fell down at Jesus' knees, saying, "Depart from me, for I am a sinful man, O Lord." For he was astonished, and all that were with him, at the catch of fish which they had taken; and so also were James and John, sons of Zebedee, who were partners with Simon. And Jesus said to Simon, "Do not be afraid; henceforth you will be catching men." And when they had brought their boats to land, they left everything and followed him.

Put Out into the Deep

What does a carpenter know about fishing? Perhaps that was what they were wondering—at least that is how I imagine it. Simon, whom Jesus then called "Peter" (the Rock), and his brother Andrew, just like the two brothers James and John, the sons of Zebedee, were fishermen by trade. They knew their work, which they had learned from their fathers. They knew when and where they had to fish in order to be successful. And they knew all about the toils and dangers of their work—like the storms that suddenly blew up and had in the past capsized many a boat. A boat like that was found a few years ago in the mud at the bottom of Lake Gennesaret. It dates from around the time of Jesus, and today it is the centerpiece of a museum on the shore of the lake.

Jesus hardly knew anything about a fisherman's life. He had grown up inland, at Nazareth. He had a quite different kind of trade. What did a carpenter know about the work of a fisherman? And now comes the amazing thing: Jesus, having climbed into their boat, urges the fishermen to put out into the deep and to throw out their nets. Although the fishermen must surely have told themselves that there was no point in doing that now, that they had already toiled all night without success, and that fish were not now suddenly going to be there in broad daylight, they nonetheless took Jesus at his word. Against all their professional experience, they gave it one more try—and made an inconceivably great catch of fish!

"Put out into the deep!" What Jesus said to Peter was taken up by Pope John Paul II (d. 2005) at the beginning of our new millennium. The Pope cried to all Christians: "Throw your nets out once more!" This call of the Pope's at the beginning of 2001 was a great surprise to me: it was not a tired, pessimistic, resigned "Nothing is ever any good" but a courageous "Put out into the deep! Dare to do it! Try it once more! Do not say, 'There is nothing to be done! We have already tried everything, and it was no use; it is just a waste of effort.'" No, the attitude of Simon Peter's successor was quite different. Like Peter, he put his trust in what Jesus said: "At your word, I will let down the nets."

The scene from today's Gospel reading can help us in many different situations. Who does not experience some moments when nothing seems to work anymore, when all the paths are blocked? It can be that way in personal relationships or in our work. A good many parishes have that kind of experience today. Despite all their efforts, everything seems to be getting more and more difficult, less and less successful. Now Jesus is saying to us, through his Gospel, through people who have had the same experience, "Give it one more try! Put your trust in me and in my help! After all, I'm in the same boat with you."

"Depart from me, for I am a sinful man, O Lord." That is how Peter reacts to the utterly unexpected catch of fish. He is scared at God's presence in Jesus. That is a wholesome scare, whenever we become aware of the greatness and the holiness of God. That may come about in some experience of nature: "My God, how great thou art!" It may be on the occasion of being saved from some serious danger: "O God, thou hast protected me beyond my deserts!" At moments like these, we know: "Now I must change my life!" Peter did that. He left everything, followed Jesus, and became a great "fisher of men". His example encourages us to trust in what Jesus says: "Put out into the deep!"

Sixth Sunday in Ordinary Time

The Gospel of Luke 6:17, 20–26

[Jesus] came down with [the Twelve] and stood on a level place, with a great crowd of his disciples and a great multitude of people from all Judea and Jerusalem and the seacoast of Tyre and Sidon, who came to hear him and to be healed of their diseases. . . .

And he lifted up his eyes on his disciples, and said:

"Blessed are you poor, for yours is the kingdom of God.

"Blessed are you that hunger now, for you shall be satisfied.

"Blessed are you that weep now, for you shall laugh.

"Blessed are you when men hate you, and when they exclude you and revile you, and cast out your name as evil, on account of the Son of man! Rejoice in that day, and leap for joy, for behold, your reward is great in heaven; for so their fathers did to the prophets.

"But woe to you that are rich, for you have received your consolation.

"Woe to you that are full now, for you shall hunger.

"Woe to you that laugh now, for you shall mourn and weep.

"Woe to you, when all men speak well of you, for so their fathers did to the false prophets."

This is no small price that Jesus expects his disciples to pay. The people whom Jesus is calling "happy"—indeed, "blessed" —are certainly not those who would be seen as being in an enviable position in normal life. And, contrariwise, Jesus utters an emphatic lament over those who are normally regarded as happy. He undertakes a complete reversal of current values. How does he come to stand current attitudes to life on their head so radically? And how are we to take this?

First, a brief historical note: the two Evangelists, Matthew and Luke, have somewhat differing versions of the so-called Sermon on the Mount. Matthew mentions eight "Beatitudes", and Luke only four; but instead the latter adds the four "laments". These differences do not mean that Jesus' words have not been reliably transmitted. Jesus talked to the people often, in many different places. In doing so, he will surely have been preaching essentially the same thing—but certainly not in the same words.

In order to understand Jesus' "reversal of all values" better, it is enough (as a first step) to put ourselves in the place in which Jesus' first disciples actually found themselves. They were indeed genuinely poor, for they had left everything in order to share in Jesus' life of want. They were genuinely hungry—and that was something they had in common with many poor people at the time (as also today). They would certainly not simply have wept, for Jesus had taught them sympathy: he taught them not to pass by want and sorrow but to weep with those who were weeping. Soon the disciples were also to be abused and brought into disrepute, like their Master himself, whom many people picked to pieces.

Jesus consoles them: you will be satisfied, and will laugh, and receive a great reward in heaven. Now you are suffering; later you will enjoy great happiness. You can already rejoice on that account now. Heaven is already shining through into your present trouble.

Karl Marx (d. 1883) and his many disciples have protested enough against that. Jesus consoles the poor and the persecuted with a distant heaven instead of changing things right now so that want and injustice disappear in this world—not merely in some "new life" or other. The Communist revolution was supposed to bring the kingdom of heaven on earth. Instead, it brought the gulags and many millions of victims who died of hunger, prison camps, persecution, and police terrorism. That was no paradise.

Today it is capitalism, triumphing worldwide, that seems to have been victorious. Its "beatitudes" are radically different from those that Jesus was proclaiming two thousand years ago. Blessed are those who are successful, it says, the speedy; blessed is the fun society; blessed are those whose name is in every mouth, those whose motto is "Heaven is where I am." Those who realize their ambitions and succeed in "Wellness" are reckoned as blessed.

Jesus does not turn his gaze away from those who are standing in the shadows of life. Nowadays, they are those who lose out in globalization, who are rationalized away and find themselves on the scrap heap as young as forty-eight; those who are orphaned by divorce; those whose handicapped lives are increasingly reckoned as "unfit for living". Jesus' call is directed to all of them today: "Society may exclude you, but in my eyes, you are completely worthwhile as people."

Those who follow Jesus have to revise their scale of values radically. Success is good, but people are more important.

Enjoying life is pleasant, but it is not everything. There are many things only trouble can teach us. I can learn a great deal if I look at the people whom Jesus called "blessed".

Seventh Sunday in Ordinary Time

The Gospel of Luke 6:27–38

"I say to you that hear, Love your enemies, do good to those who hate you, bless those who curse you, pray for those who abuse you. To him who strikes you on the cheek, offer the other also; and from him who takes away your cloak do not withhold your coat as well. Give to every one who begs from you; and of him who takes away your goods do not ask them again. And as you wish that men would do to you, do so to them.

"If you love those who love you, what credit is that to you? For even sinners love those who love them. And if you do good to those who do good to you, what credit is that to you? For even sinners do the same. And if you lend to those from whom you hope to receive, what credit is that to you? Even sinners lend to sinners, to receive as much again. But love your enemies, and do good, and lend, expecting nothing in return; and your reward will be great, and you will be sons of the Most High; for he is kind to the ungrateful and the selfish. Be merciful, even as your Father is merciful.

"Judge not, and you will not be judged; condemn not, and you will not be condemned; forgive, and you will be forgiven; give, and it will be given to you; good measure, pressed down, shaken together, running over, will be put into your lap. For the measure you give will be the measure you get back."

At first glance, it seems impossible: holding out the other cheek as well. We are supposed to love our enemies? That is asking far too much. Doing good to those who hate us: who has the strength for that? I am supposed to bless those who curse me? Is all that not unnatural? How can we get on in life if we never defend ourselves? Is injustice supposed to be allowed free rein? What would become of us if the state were to be governed by the words of Jesus? What does a country look like in which crime is no longer punished?

Of course, these sayings of Jesus are not concerned with the state. The state has to punish crimes appropriately. Otherwise it is opening the door wide to crime. What is this about, then? This is talking about me, about my personal attitude. This is the question—so decisive for my life—of whether I really love my neighbor.

What Jesus is asking of us is basically something quite simple, which he has summarized in a positive sense in the so-called Golden Rule: "As you wish that men would do to you, do so to them." It is therefore enough, in any situation, to ask what I expect from other people and how I hope they will treat me, in order to grasp what I should do or leave undone. I need only to picture for myself how I would like people to deal with me in a certain situation in order to have a quite practical guide as to how I should behave.

For example, when I am angry, quite worked up, "my hand has slipped"—perhaps not literally but in a figurative sense. I have really rebuked a colleague, a neighbor, or whomever it might be. And now I find that the person concerned does not pay me back in kind, does not strike back. I am amazed, and my anger evaporates; the friendliness of the person I attacked disarms me. Through the way that the other person held out his left cheek, too, so to speak, the spiral of violence has been interrupted. I am grateful that the other person did not allow himself to be carried away and take revenge. What it looks like when the deadly round of violence and counterviolence, of revenge and the avenging of revenge just keeps right on turning is something we see day by day in the afflicted Holy Land.

Yet Jesus does not merely teach us to refrain from striking back. He refers us to the root whence springs the strength we need for refraining. This is, quite purely and simply, love. But what kind of love? Not the selfish kind, which is thinking only of what it gets in return. Not "interested" love, which is looking above all toward what will come of this or that. It is not hard to like only those who like me. Giving only in cases in which I am sure that a count will be kept and that I will receive a plentiful recompense—all that is still not really love. It is, rather, something done for a purpose, from cold calculation—not from generosity. Yet this is a matter of generosity. And mercy is a part of it, too: not scrupulously reckoning other people's mistakes but applying to others the same measure by which I myself would like to be measured. Anyone who knows himself just a little bit knows how very much each of us needs the benefit of a merciful standard.

And that is what God applies to us. If he did not do so, we would be lost. God looks kindly upon even ungrateful people, although they do not deserve it. By using only this yardstick can we love our enemies—not the evil they have done to us but the humans they still are in spite of that. Do not we too want to be regarded as humans, as children of God, despite our mistakes?

Eighth Sunday in Ordinary Time

The Gospel of Luke 6:39–45

[Jesus] told [his disciples] a parable: "Can a blind man lead a blind man? Will they not both fall into a pit? A disciple is not above his teacher, but every one when he is fully taught will be like his teacher. Why do you see the speck that is in your brother's eye, but do not notice the log that is in your own eye? Or how can you say to your brother, 'Brother, let me take out the speck that is in your eye,' when you yourself do not see the log that is in your own eye? You hypocrite, first take the log out of your own eye, and then you will see clearly to take out the speck that is in your brother's eye.

"For no good tree bears bad fruit, nor again does a bad tree bear good fruit; for each tree is known by its own fruit. For figs are not gathered from thorns, nor are grapes picked from a bramble bush. The good man out of the good treasure of his heart produces good, and the evil man out of his evil treasure produces evil; for out of the abundance of the heart his mouth speaks."

What the Heart Is Full of . . .

Like so many of Jesus' sayings, this too has become a proverb: "What the heart is full of spills out of the mouth" (or "the mouth will speak of"). Probably, however, Jesus himself was using a well-known proverb here. The same is true of the other aphorisms in this section of the "sermon on the plain" (Lk 6:20–49), which represents a counterpart in Luke's Gospel to the Sermon on the Mount in the Gospel of Matthew (Mt 5–7).

Time and again, the Lord refers to everyday experience, to popular wisdom. Blind men cannot lead blind men—anyone can see that. You can recognize the quality of a tree by its fruit, and that of a person by his deeds.

If that is all obvious in any case, then why make a point of talking about it? What is new about what Jesus is saying? Where is there a divine revelation here if human wisdom already knows about this?

Christ did not just say entirely new things. What he says reveals a great deal that we could well know for ourselves—but are all too keen to suppress. There is nowhere that this game of hiding things becomes clearer than in flattery. There is no false behavior that Jesus tackles so severely as pretense, false appearances, acting "as if". Today's section from the Gospel turns around the unmasking and the healing of hypocrisy.

Where does it come from, this game of masks, misrepresenting oneself? The Lord, who is an incomparable "head-shrinker", talks first of all about the symptoms of this mental ulcer. And yet, as a good doctor, the best of all doctors, he penetrates to the roots of this syndrome. Let us look first at the sickness, and then at its origins.

Blind men are trying to lead other blind men. They think they can see, and yet they are blind. How often do we think we know better, reading someone else the riot act, without knowing ourselves? We all have to put this question to ourselves: If I have to guide other people—children, in the family; colleagues, at work; the fate of society, in politics—

can I see well enough, am I sufficiently farsighted and clear-sighted, to show the way to others?

How can I begin to see? By beginning with my eyes! The proverbial picture of a plank in one's own eye is a drastic one. "You don't see your own gigantic mistakes, but you criticize other people's little failings. Get more clear-sighted about yourself first. Look at your blind spots, on account of which you overlook those things in yourself that anyone could tell you about, if you were ready to accept honest criticism!"

Blindness about oneself has more profound roots. How do things look in my heart? What is it full of? Of lust and meanness, jealousy and envy? Our mouths cannot lie in the long run. Whatever is in our hearts slips out again through our mouths, after all—even if only in asides.

Truth will catch up with us. Our mouths betray what is in our hearts, and our deeds show what kind of tree we are. Hypocrisy cannot stand the strain—and that is a good thing. The truth hurts. But it sets us free. And then Jesus, the good doctor, can heal our hearts, too, and plant his love in them. Only Jesus can make our hearts like his.

Ninth Sunday in Ordinary Time

The Gospel of Luke 7:1–10

After he had ended all his sayings in the hearing of the people [Jesus] entered Capernaum. Now a centurion had a slave who was dear to him, who was sick and at the point of death. When he heard of Jesus, he sent to him elders of the Jews, asking him to come and heal his slave. And when they came to Jesus, they begged him earnestly, saying, "He is worthy to have you do this for him, for he loves our nation, and he built us our synagogue." And Jesus went with them. When he was not far from the house, the centurion sent friends to him, saying to him, "Lord, do not trouble yourself, for I am not worthy to have you come under my roof; therefore I did not presume to come to you. But say the word, and let my servant be healed. For I am a man set under authority, with soldiers under me: and I say to one, 'Go,' and he goes; and to another, 'Come,' and he comes; and to my slave, 'Do this,' and he does it." When Jesus heard this he marveled at him, and turned and said to the multitude that followed him, "I tell you, not even in Israel have I found such faith." And when those who had been sent returned to the house, they found the slave well.

"Lord, I am not worthy that you should enter under my roof, but only say the word and my soul shall be healed." At each Holy Mass, these words* are spoken when the priest shows the people the Host, saying as he does so, "Behold the Lamb of God, who takes away the sins of the world."

I am not sure whether all the people who hear these words, and speak them, even recall whence they come. The somewhat old-fashioned form of speech may further hinder their understanding. What does "enter under my roof" mean? Anyone who has a roof over his head has his own home, his living-quarters. "Enter under my roof" means "Come into my home". Who is it who is not to come in? Jesus himself! For he himself is present in the Host. I know that I am not worthy to receive him under my roof. Who can say of himself that he has deserved this and that it is appropriate that Jesus himself should come to him as a guest?

We find the model for this attitude in today's Gospel reading. A captain in the Roman army of occupation has heard about Jesus. Although the captain is used to giving orders, to "ordering his people about", he does not regard himself as worthy to command Jesus to come to him. He sends some Jewish dignitaries to Jesus to put in a good word for him and to commend him as a friend.

As Jesus is nearing the officer's house, the latter once more shows his modesty. He does not come to meet Jesus himself. He sends friends to tell Jesus that he need not take the trouble to come into his house. What delicacy of feeling! For he

* At the date of publication, these words in the English translation for the Mass are rendered differently: "Lord, I am not worthy to receive you, but only say the word and I shall be healed."—Ed.

obviously knew that it was forbidden for a believing Jew to go into a pagan's house.

What is still more astonishing, however, is the arrangement he suggests: "A single word from you will be enough, and my mortally ill servant will get well." How on earth did he come to such unshakable faith? He knows that when he gives a soldier an order, then what he has commanded will be done. Why should it be different with Jesus, who has far more power than he has as a simple captain?

Only in two cases have expressions of Jesus' astonishment at faith in him been passed down. In both cases, the people were pagans. "O woman, great is your faith!" says Jesus in admiration to the Canaanite woman who was not to be deterred from her petition by anything at all (Mt 15:21–28). "Not even in Israel have I found such faith", says Jesus about the captain.

Does he find that kind of faith in our case? It must have been an indescribable joy for Jesus to encounter a pure and genuine attitude of faith. What is the loveliest thing about this attitude? I think it is, above all, the trust that finds its expression here. Faith trusts in God to do great things. And it is thereby giving honor to God; it is recognizing that God is God. Ultimately, such a trust can stem only from love. Anyone who, like the captain, trusts in Jesus to act with God's power and his mercy is also showing genuine love for him. And that is exactly what the first commandment demands of us: to love God with all our hearts. Will Jesus find faith like this among us? Yes, if we truly love him!

Tenth Sunday in Ordinary Time

The Gospel of Luke 7:11–17

Soon afterward [Jesus] went to a city called Nain, and his disciples and a great crowd went with him. As he drew near to the gate of the city, behold, a man who had died was being carried out, the only son of his mother, and she was a widow; and a large crowd from the city was with her. And when the Lord saw her, he had compassion on her and said to her, "Do not weep." And he came and touched the bier, and the bearers stood still. And he said, "Young man, I say to you, arise." And the dead man sat up, and began to speak. And he gave him to his mother. Fear seized them all; and they glorified God, saying, "A great prophet has arisen among us!" and "God has visited his people!" And this report concerning him spread through the whole of Judea and all the surrounding country.

Terminus: Life

Is not the whole story of mankind like a long, endless funeral procession? Thousands of people are carried to their graves every day. Everywhere, there is mourning—which is often heartbreaking. Mothers weep for their sons who have been killed in war. I am always upset by the war memorials—dozens of names in even the smallest village, often with pictures, of young men carried off by the utter lunacy of war—and how many tears there are behind each one of those names!

When we die "full of days" (as the Bible says [in Job 42:17]), it is often like being set free. Yet how often death is the grim reaper, blindly mowing people down with his deadly scythe. Illnesses, accidents, catastrophes—he seems to leave no opportunity untaken to gather in his deadly harvest.

We meet one of these countless funeral processions in today's Gospel reading. The bier is just being carried out through the city gate. The dead have no place in the city of the living. They have to be given a tomb outside the walls. Behind the bier walks the mother of the dead youth, her only son; and she is a widow. How many such mothers have been widowed by war! (And how many women have to bring up their child alone today.) Behind the widow comes "a large crowd from the city".

And then the funeral procession meets another kind of procession, with Jesus at the head, his disciples behind him, and "a great crowd" besides. The two movements meet one another outside the city gate. The dead man is being carried out of the city, and Jesus is going to enter it. A simple "traffic problem"? A matter of impatient waiting, as when a motorist coming down a village street meets a funeral procession that stops him from getting on quickly?

No impatience, but sympathy: at one glance, with the understanding of his heart, Jesus grasps the misery and sorrow of this mother who is standing alone. "Seized with compassion in his inmost parts" (as we might translate literally), he addresses the woman: "Do not weep." He does not say this to her because he finds her tears a nuisance but because he is the One who "will wipe away every tear" after he has finally conquered death, when in heaven "neither shall there be mourning nor crying nor pain any more" (Rev 21:4).

The funeral procession meets up with Life. He who could say of himself, "I am the way, and the truth, and the life" (John 14:6) brings to a halt the progression toward the graveyard. "The bearers stood still." Jesus went up to the bier. Life takes the hand of the dead man. His word is enough to conquer death: "Young man, I say to you, arise."

What an impressive picture! Someone comes along who is able to put a stop to the endless funeral procession of human history. Here is someone on our way, in our town, in our world, who is able to command death to halt.

"All very well," we may say, "and marvelous that the mother gets her son back. But at some time or other they both still have to die—as we all do, even those whose lives have been saved. The funeral procession will continue, inexorably. It carries everyone along, with no exceptions." That is all true; and yet it is not everything. That same Jesus who stopped the funeral procession at the city gate of Nain, then, has not done away with death, but he has opened the city gate of heaven. All our funeral processions do not come to an end at the grave. That is only somewhere we halt on the way; the terminus is called "life" and not "death". What happened at the city gate of Nain was a taste of this, a pledge of assurance, so to speak, that this is how it will be.

Eleventh Sunday in Ordinary Time

The Gospel of Luke 7:36–50

One of the Pharisees asked [Jesus] to eat with him, and he went into the Pharisee's house, and sat at table. And behold, a woman of the city, who was a sinner, when she learned that he was sitting at table in the Pharisee's house, brought an alabaster flask of ointment, and standing behind him at his feet, weeping, she began to wet his feet with her tears, and wiped them with the hair of her head, and kissed his feet, and anointed them with the ointment. Now when the Pharisee who had invited him saw it, he said to himself, "If this man were a prophet, he would have known who and what sort of woman this is who is touching him, for she is a sinner." And Jesus answering said to him, "Simon, I have something to say to you." And he answered, "What is it, Teacher?" "A certain creditor had two debtors; one owed five hundred denarii, and the other fifty. When they could not pay, he forgave them both. Now which of them will love him more?" Simon answered, "The one, I suppose, to whom he forgave more." And he said to him, "You have judged rightly." Then turning toward the woman he said to Simon, "Do you see this woman? I entered your house, you gave me no water for my feet, but she has wet my feet with her tears and wiped them with her hair. You gave me no kiss, but from the time I came in she has not ceased to kiss my feet. You did not anoint my head with oil, but she has anointed my feet with ointment. Therefore I tell you, her sins, which are many, are forgiven, for she loved much; but he who is forgiven little, loves little." And he said to her, "Your sins are forgiven." Then those who were at table with him began to say among themselves, "Who is this, who even forgives sins?" And he said to the woman, "Your faith has saved you; go in peace."

Love—Different, for Once

You have to make the scene come alive for yourself. A banquet in the East, with the guests (men only) lying on couches, turned toward the table with their feet stretched out behind them, leaning on their left hands while they eat with their right (without cutlery). The houses stand open; servants and onlookers are crowding around the people at table.

The host is a well-known Pharisee—that is to say, a strictly practicing Jew. He has personally invited Jesus to his banquet, even though the Pharisees, pious people who were careful to keep the law, had a good many bones to pick with Jesus; indeed, some of them so radically rejected him that a few were even plotting to bring about his death (see Mt 26:4). Simon seems nonetheless to have felt a certain sympathy with Jesus—otherwise he would not have invited him to his house.

So there they are, lying around the table. The meal has started. Then a woman who is regarded in the town as a sinner pushes her way in. What was her sin? Luke, the Gospel writer, does not say, but everyone has his own ideas on this. That attitude has not changed, right to this day. "That kind of sinner"—that is the way people talk about those who sin against the sixth commandment.

What this sinner does next is shocking to everyone there. Even for our own indifferent age, when there are no more taboos, her behavior is offensive. I always try to imagine how we "men of the Church" would react today if a "sinner" came up to us in the way this woman did to Jesus.

She came up to Jesus from behind, as he was lying on the divan with his feet bare. She has brought some expensive oil with her—in the heat of the East, this is important for one's skin and does it good. Above all, however, there is a flood of tears—she is weeping and weeping. Her tears run down over Jesus' feet, and Jesus lets it happen. This woman who has sinned is not repugnant to him, and he does not repulse her when she touches him; he does not stop her when she dries his feet with her long hair. The other people are up in arms over these erotic gestures. Perhaps Jesus has no idea at all of what kind of woman she is?

Jesus does know; and he knows, too, what Simon and the others are thinking to themselves—in that imagination in which many erotic things find a place, despite every pious intention. No: here, just for once, it is not a matter of sex and eroticism, not a matter of men's desires and of "love for sale". This concerns the love that this woman had previously been seeking in vain. Here is someone who does not desire her as an object of lust but can recognize in this woman's actions and her tears the most profound longing for love, the longing for the one person who is able to give her in return the kind of love that does not leave her heart still hungry and empty.

Simon is given perhaps the most important lesson of his life—and we, too, along with him, if we listen and open up our hearts. "Simon, and all of you who are constantly judging other people, just finally understand: love is all that counts in life—real, genuine love, which knows that I, too, have been forgiven an infinite number of things. Even if I have not become a whore, have not murdered anyone, have not become a thief or a robber, this is not because I am so much better than whores or robbers but because God has been gracious to me and has kept me from it." Do I love him suitably for that?

Twelfth Sunday in Ordinary Time

The Gospel of Luke 9:18–24

Now it happened that as he was praying alone the disciples were with him; and he asked them, "Who do the people say that I am?" And they answered, "John the Baptist; but others say, Elijah; and others, that one of the old prophets has risen." And he said to them, "But who do you say that I am?" And Peter answered, "The Christ of God." But he charged and commanded them to tell this to no one, saying, "The Son of man must suffer many things, and be rejected by the elders and chief priests and scribes, and be killed, and on the third day be raised."

And he said to all, "If any man would come after me, let him deny himself and take up his cross daily and follow me. For whoever would save his life will lose it; and whoever loses his life for my sake, he will save it."

Who Is He?

This scene remained unforgettable in the memory of the Apostles. They must have recounted it often. Three of the four Gospels report it, Matthew in the greatest detail. The place where it happened was off the beaten track, a lonely place near Caesarea Philippi in the north of Galilee, close to the springs of the Jordan. Luke highlights the fact that in this lonely place Jesus was devoting his attention mainly to prayer.

At this quiet time, away from everything, Jesus openly expressed a question that had been on his companions' minds ever since they had met him: Who was he really? What was there behind the carpenter from Nazareth? This question obviously preoccupied the people who had met him. Every possible view of this was circulating. The views have one thing in common: Jesus is someone special, a man of God like John the Baptist, a prophet like Elijah or like one of those prophets from earlier centuries.

To this day, most people's opinions run in that direction. Islam sees in Jesus a great and important prophet. Many people regard him as a kind of religious genius, an admirable person—as being, along with Buddha, Moses, Muhammad, and others, one of the great founders of religions.

"But who do you say that I am?" This question is no longer being put to public opinion; it has become quite personal: "You have been on the road with me all this time, you have left your work and your families, to share with me a difficult and uncertain itinerant life. You have followed me up to now, you have come to know my way of life; you have heard what I say to people, and you have seen how blind people see again, lame people walk, and even the dead are raised up. What do you think of me, after all that?"

"We think you are the Messiah!" replies Peter, without hesitation. "In fact, we have thought that all along, since we first got to know you." At first it was a question, and now it has become a certainty: "You are the One for whom our people have been waiting for generations, the One who was promised, who comes to save us and set us free; you are God's anointed one (that is what the word "Messiah" means), the Christ (the Greek word for the "Anointed One", the Messiah).

At last it has been said out in the open. Everything is clear now. Jesus reaffirms it—in the future they will know where they are. And yet hardly has it been said when there comes an unexpected twist. Instead of talking about what they all expected from the coming Messiah in those days—about peace and liberation, about the end of all suffering and weeping—Jesus talks about sufferings that lie ahead of him, about persecution and death, and—most mysteriously—about a Resurrection.

And besides that, if his companions wish to follow him any further, they have to be similarly ready to take trouble and suffering upon themselves. They had not imagined the Messiah like that: they really had expected something quite different from him, something quite different for themselves.

Nonetheless, they were willing to commit themselves. They soon discovered that the path that Jesus had pointed out for them was the only right way. It proved its value in ordinary life. They found by experience that Jesus was right: whoever denies himself every day, anyone who struggles, day by day, to overcome his weaknesses, to take his labors upon himself, to carry his cross (and who goes through life without any cross at all?)—that person will find that in doing so, he is not left alone: the Messiah, the Christ, the Savior, will be with him. He truly is, to this day, the One who saves.

Thirteenth Sunday in Ordinary Time

The Gospel of Luke 9:51–62

When the days drew near for him to be received up, he set his face to go to Jerusalem. And he sent messengers ahead of him, who went and entered a village of the Samaritans, to make ready for him; but the people would not receive him, because his face was set toward Jerusalem. And when his disciples James and John saw it, they said, "Lord, do you want us to bid fire come down from heaven and consume them?" But he turned and rebuked them. And they went on to another village.

As they were going along the road, a man said to him, "I will follow you wherever you go." And Jesus said to him, "Foxes have holes, and birds of the air have nests; but the Son of man has nowhere to lay his head." To another he said, "Follow me." But he said, "Lord, let me first go and bury my father." But he said to him, "Leave the dead to bury their own dead; but as for you, go and proclaim the kingdom of God." Another said, "I will follow you, Lord; but let me first say farewell to those at my home." Jesus said to him, "No one who puts his hand to the plow and looks back is fit for the kingdom of God."

I Have Not Regretted It

In decided fashion, Jesus goes his way. Who wants to go with him? Life is a road we travel, and we are always on the move, as long as we live. Not until the end of our lives do we reach the goal, through the narrow gate of death.

But how do we go on our way—hastily or peacefully, hesitantly or in decided fashion? Is there a goal we should reach? Do we know about this goal? Or are our lives just a matter of stumbling on from one day to the next? Are our lives a matter of laboriously "muddling through", alternating between duty and entertainment, between tasks and amusements? It may be even worse—our lives may appear to us as empty, meaningless, and without sure foundation. Then we are liable to take to drinking alcohol, in order to forget, and liable to despair to the point of suicide.

How important it is, therefore, to meet people in life who can give us some sense of direction, people who know what they want themselves and can carry others along with them so as to give their lives a direction and a goal. That is one thing about Jesus that has always fascinated people. He was able to be a fingerpost, to show the meaning of life, and he has been for many people a model worthy of emulation.

In today's Gospel reading, we meet some people who are trying to do this. Some of them have been with him on the road for quite a while; they are his enthusiastic supporters, almost fanatics, because when people will not offer them a welcome in a Samaritan village, they want to declare a "holy war" right away and conjure up fire to fall upon that inhospitable village.

Samaritans did not like Jews, and any Jews who passed through their area on their way to Jerusalem as pilgrims had to reckon with their hostility. Jesus' disciples still do not seem to have learned much from their Master when they demand a fiery and bloodthirsty revenge. Jesus speaks very sharply to them: he has not come to make people his slaves with fire and sword. His goal is Jerusalem, for it is there that he intends to give up his life for men—not to compel them to do anything but to free them from the compulsion of sin. That is what they have to learn from him so as to become like him themselves.

Time and again, people come to meet them, wanting to join him on his way. Three are mentioned in particular, and they stand for many others who, up to this day, are contemplating following Jesus more explicitly, becoming completely his disciples. Jesus seems to set the bar so high for that that we can hardly be surprised if many of them lose courage or do not even make a start at following him. Jesus points out every conceivable difficulty that life in close companionship with him may bring: Jesus, the Son of man, is homeless upon earth. "Are you ready to accept that for yourself? If you want to go along with me, then do not look back but commit yourself wholly to my path."

Did those three then follow Jesus, in fact? The Gospel does not tell us. Yet it is a fact that for the past two thousand years, countless men and women have committed themselves to the thrilling adventure of discipleship. In particular, these have often been (and still are) young people who are seized by the call of Jesus. He drew me as a young man. And in spite of all my own weaknesses, I have not for one moment regretted, to this day, having followed him.

Fourteenth Sunday in Ordinary Time

The Gospel of Luke 10:1–12, 17–20

After this the Lord appointed seventy others, and sent them on ahead of him, two by two, into every town and place where he himself was about to come. And he said to them, "The harvest is plentiful, but the laborers are few; pray therefore the Lord of the harvest to send out laborers into his harvest. Go your way; behold, I send you out as lambs in the midst of wolves. Carry no purse, no bag, no sandals; and salute no one on the road. Whatever house you enter, first say, 'Peace be to this house!' And if a son of peace is there, your peace shall rest upon him; but if not, it shall return to you. And remain in the same house, eating and drinking what they provide, for the laborer deserves his wages; do not go from house to house. Whenever you enter a town and they receive you, eat what is set before you; heal the sick in it and say to them, 'The kingdom of God has come near to you.' But whenever you enter a town and they do not receive you, go into its streets and say, 'Even the dust of your town that clings to our feet, we wipe off against you; nevertheless know this, that the kingdom of God has come near.' I tell you, it shall be more tolerable on that day for Sodom than for that town." . . .*

The seventy returned with joy, saying, "Lord, even the demons are subject to us in your name!" And he said to them, "I saw Satan fall like lightning from heaven. Behold, I have given you authority to tread upon serpents*

* The Revised Standard Version of the Bible reads seventy, but it indicates in a footnote that other ancient authorities read seventy-two.—Ed.

and scorpions, and over all the power of the enemy; and nothing shall hurt you. Nevertheless do not rejoice in this, that the spirits are subject to you; but rejoice that your names are written in heaven."

It Is Harvest Time!

When the harvest is ripe, you have to hurry. You cannot wait around. Time presses. If the harvest is not brought in promptly, then it will spoil. It rots and perishes.

We can feel the urgency and sense of emergency in Jesus' words, "The harvest is plentiful, but the laborers are few." He can see how ripe the fields are and that there is a dramatic shortage of harvesters.

What harvest are we talking about, and what workers?

The field in which the harvest is waiting to be brought in is pretty big: it is the whole earth. Jesus has in mind not merely the little patch of the world in which he lives, his home province of Galilee, or the Holy Land. Right from the start, he is concerned with the entire world. His message is to be taken to all peoples; it is meant for all men. That is why he is sending his messengers into all the countries of the world.

In the Jewish conceptions of that period, there were seventy-two nations upon earth. That is why Jesus chose, in addition to the Twelve, "seventy-two others, and sent them on ahead of him, two by two, into every town and place where he himself was about to come." At first it is only a matter of their preparing for the arrival of Jesus in all the places in Galilee. They are supposed to prepare the ground for him and help him in his "tour" through Galilee. But that is only the beginning. Later on, it will be a matter of going to all the countries of the earth to prepare the ground for Jesus, for up to this day his intention is to come to all men with his message of reconciliation and love.

Even then, when he first sent out missionaries, Jesus gave them clear rules for the mission. Wherever they have kept to them, in the course of the centuries, a blessing has come of it. When they have not, then often there were serious abuses and distortions.

Today, the question of mission is once more clearly posed for us, as a challenge. Everywhere on our globe, religions and doctrines of salvation are proceeding upon their missions: Christian groups and churches, Islam, the Asiatic religions, and even ideologies (let us recall how Communism intended to conquer the world) and philosophies of life. But how is "mission" being undertaken by all these forces? By compulsion, oppression, and power? Or with a great respect for people's consciences and for each individual's freedom?

Jesus gave his missionaries clear instructions—not to be like ravening wolves but the very opposite: "I send you out as lambs in the midst of wolves." Year after year, all over the world, missionaries are killed simply because they stand up for the poor and people with no rights or because they are bringing the Gospel into people's midst.

Jesus himself lived as a poor man and trusted in God's providence. That is also what he wanted his missionaries to do. This example being lived out has often been more convincing than any words. To this day, this is the most convincing route missions can take. I am thinking of someone like Bishop Erwin Kräutler among the Indians on the Amazon, and of many less well-known people who are quite simply living out the love of Christ among men.

For Jesus, it is urgent that many people should become enthusiastic about him and allow themselves to be sent out, for the harvest is enormous. There just cannot be enough workers there to bring in the harvest. Can we not see how far our world is truly overripe for the Good News of Jesus?

Fifteenth Sunday in Ordinary Time

The Gospel of Luke 10:25–37

And behold, a lawyer stood up to put [Jesus] to the test, saying, "Teacher, what shall I do to inherit eternal life?" He said to him, "What is written in the law? What do you read?" And he answered, "You shall love the Lord your God with all your heart, and with all your soul, and with all your strength, and with all your mind; and your neighbor as yourself." And he said to him, "You have answered right; do this, and you will live."

But he, desiring to justify himself, said to Jesus, "And who is my neighbor?" Jesus replied, "A man was going down from Jerusalem to Jericho, and he fell among robbers, who stripped him and beat him, and departed, leaving him half dead. Now by chance a priest was going down that road; and when he saw him he passed by on the other side. So likewise a Levite, when he came to the place and saw him, passed by on the other side. But a Samaritan, as he journeyed, came to where he was; and when he saw him, he had compassion, and went to him and bound up his wounds, pouring on oil and wine; then he set him on his own beast and brought him to an inn, and took care of him. And the next day he took out two denarii and gave them to the innkeeper, saying, 'Take care of him; and whatever more you spend, I will repay you when I come back.' Which of these three, do you think, proved neighbor to the man who fell among the robbers?" He said, "The one who showed mercy on him." And Jesus said to him, "Go and do likewise."

The Samaritan

The good Samaritan is among those figures in the Gospel that have become proverbial. This finds expression, for example, in the charitable organization of the Workers' Samaritan Association. Who is this traveler who did not pass by his neighbor's need with indifference and ignore it?

We begin with a typical theological discussion, the kind held even today: discussion for the sake of discussion, putting forth trick questions intended to embarrass the other person, and choosing subjects that are of immediate interest or are fashionable. At any rate, at that time it was the question of how someone could attain eternal life. Nowadays, where religion and the Church are concerned, it is often far more superficial questions that people address, such as those concerning the Inquisition, Catholic sexual morality, or the Church's wealth.

Jesus gives the discussion an entirely personal twist: it is not a matter of what people actually say, and not even of what is in the Bible, but simply and solely of whether you act and live accordingly. Suddenly, this is no longer a general discussion with no implications for anyone, but a discussion that is entirely personal to me.

"Who is my neighbor?" Love of one's neighbor, which is indivisible from love of God—what does it look like? The story that Jesus tells has the answer in itself. To this day, it is still a hard nut to crack. The priest is in a hurry. He is coming away from his duty in the temple at Jerusalem and wants to get home. Perhaps he is afraid of the robbers who have been responsible for leaving this man lying half-dead on the side of the road. Perhaps they are lying in wait for their next victim.

So the best thing is to get on. See nothing, hear nothing, and leave quickly. The Levite who comes after him—in a lower rank of spiritual office—follows the sad example of his spiritual superior.

The "full-time" religious people are not portrayed well in Jesus' story. That remains for them (for us clergy!) a constant and serious warning. The Samaritan, who does not pass the wounded man by, is a stranger, a foreigner. In those days, in Israel, the Samaritans were looked upon as enemies of the people, and their religion was rejected as being semi-pagan. It is one of these very people that Jesus offers as a model. The Samaritan interrupts his journey; he does not (as we would say nowadays) look at the clock, nor in his appointment book. Here is a man in danger of his life. Help is urgently needed, and without hesitation he gives first aid, basic treatment for the wounds; only when he knows the victim is being looked after at an inn does he continue his journey.

A few years ago, I was privileged to take part in an ecumenical celebration for the blessing of the new center of the Workers' Samaritan Association. I was also asked to bless an icon, which had been painted by a Russian clergyman, for the chief's office. The icon portrayed the good Samaritan. And now, the surprising thing: the Samaritan had the face of Jesus Christ. The explanation of the icon painter was that Christ himself is the Samaritan, and we are the wounded man. Jesus does not overlook our need. He helps us and heals us and brings us home into his Father's inn. He thus shows himself to be truly our neighbor. "Go and do likewise!"

Sixteenth Sunday in Ordinary Time

The Gospel of Luke 10:38–42

Now as they went on their way, [Jesus] entered a village; and a woman named Martha received him into her house. And she had a sister called Mary, who sat at the Lord's feet and listened to his teaching. But Martha was distracted with much serving; and she went to him and said, "Lord, do you not care that my sister has left me to serve alone? Tell her then to help me." But the Lord answered her, "Martha, Martha, you are anxious and troubled about many things; one thing is needful. Mary has chosen the good portion, which shall not be taken away from her."

Windows for Vacation Time

The Gospel is always like a mirror and like a window: a mirror, because it shows me how things are in my life, and where I am in danger of going astray; and a window, because it opens up a new vista to me, offering a brightly lit view into the distance and showing me a path full of hope.

Martha and Mary, the two sisters, stand for two different attitudes, two approaches to life. Let us look first of all in the mirror they hold up to us, so that a window may be opened for us in a new direction. Martha, the sister of Mary, is the hostess. She is the enterprising one, the active sister. She welcomes Jesus into her house, offering him rest after his travel, a stopping place on his journey to Jerusalem. She sees to his comfort. From the few words Luke uses to describe the scene in his Gospel, we can imagine that she is industriously and somewhat hectically busy looking after her guest. She is radiating disturbance from sheer enthusiasm and is making a lot of bother for herself and her guest.

It is different with Mary: she sits down by Jesus, at his feet. She listens to him. She has time entirely for him and is full of interest in him. Martha has welcomed Jesus into her home, but Mary welcomes him into her heart. She makes him a gift, not of her activity, but of her attention.

Is not the praise Jesus gives her unjust? If Martha just sat there, like Mary, then who would take care of the meal? Who would set the table? It is all very well to listen, but work will not wait, and the table will not set itself full of food and drink. Martha's annoyance with her sister is only too comprehensible. Jesus holds a mirror up to her: "You are taking a great deal of trouble. But you are in danger of forgetting the most essential thing. What use is all the trouble and anxiety if amid it all you have no longer any time for me? What use is your hospitality if you are wearing yourself out and we can no longer talk to each other at all?"

I can see myself in this mirror. Let us have the confidence to look into it! "Activism" is the great danger of our age. Something always has to be happening, from one event to another—even on vacation. The carousel of our day planner spins around ever faster, while our life becomes more and more hectic. I have to come to everything—just not to myself. Time is squeezed in for everything, and only time for God goes short. If the feeling of "running empty" increasingly bothers us, is it surprising that many people feel burned out?

And here the Gospel opens a window. Jesus points to Martha's sister Mary: "Mary has chosen the good portion."

Seeing to things and taking trouble are not bad, but they should not swallow everything up. It is necessary to be active, but it stands in need of contemplation, of tranquillity, of reflection and prayer as a sound basis. Such people do exist: extremely active and yet not hectically busy, ready to help and at the same time ready to listen. Their secret is that they give enough time to God; they listen to his word; they draw strength and peace from prayer. They are the really helpful people. Busyness helps no one. Now, in the vacation period, it is time to take time, like Mary, to listen to Jesus in all tranquillity.

Seventeenth Sunday in Ordinary Time

The Gospel of Luke 11:1–13

[Jesus] was praying in a certain place, and when he ceased, one of his disciples said to him, "Lord, teach us to pray, as John taught his disciples." And he said to them, "When you pray, say:

"Father, hallowed be your name. Your kingdom come. Give us each day our daily bread; and forgive us our sins, for we ourselves forgive every one who is indebted to us; and lead us not into temptation."

And he said to them, "Which of you who has a friend will go to him at midnight and say to him, 'Friend, lend me three loaves; for a friend of mine has arrived on a journey, and I have nothing to set before him'; and he will answer from within, 'Do not bother me; the door is now shut, and my children are with me in bed; I cannot get up and give you anything'? I tell you, though he will not get up and give him anything because he is his friend, yet because of his importunity he will rise and give him whatever he needs. And I tell you, Ask, and it will be given you; seek, and you will find; knock, and it will be opened to you. For every one who asks receives, and he who seeks finds, and to him who knocks it will be opened. What father among you, if his son asks for a fish, will instead of a fish give him a serpent; or if he asks for an egg, will give him a scorpion? If you then, who are evil, know how to give good gifts to your children, how much more will the heavenly Father give the Holy Spirit to those who ask him!"

Teach Us to Pray!

It is one of the things that make the strongest impression on me—watching someone who has sunk deep down into prayer. It is probably not just for me that this is so. The impression that Saint Padre Pio (d. 1968) made on me—a seventeen-year-old at the time—is unforgettable. And many people found Pope John Paul II, as someone once said, "a rock of prayer". But we need not go so far afield. We find people who pray, here around us, in churches and sometimes even on the subway.

What is the mysterious thing that is happening there? What happens within a person who is praying—within the Muslim I saw at the airport in Rome, for instance, simply spreading out his little carpet and then quietly praying, undisturbed by the crowd?

Whenever Jesus prayed, that must have made a deep impression on his disciples. They often saw him praying—sometimes all night long. What was he doing? What happened within him? In today's Gospel reading, we see him praying once again, somewhere or other. The place makes no difference. His prayer is the only interesting thing. Nobody dares to disturb him then. Only after he himself has finished praying, one of them ventures to ask him what they have all had on their minds for a long time: We want to learn that, too! Tell us, show us how you do it—how we can do it.

The best person to teach about praying is someone who prays himself. When children "catch" their parents praying, that often makes an impression that influences their whole lives: "So praying is not just something for children to do before going to sleep. It is something so important that even our parents do it." The disciples did not learn in theory how important prayer is but in quite concrete fashion, seeing Jesus himself. They found that, for their Master, it was something vitally important.

And now the surprising thing: Jesus did not give his disciples a course on the theory of prayer or on methods of learning to pray. Nor does he tell them how he prays himself. That remains his personal secret. It is as if he were trying to tell them, "Praying can be learned only by praying! But if you do want to pray, then do it in these words"—and then follows the Our Father.

Luke transmits to us a shorter form of this, probably the most famous of all prayers. Matthew gives us the version that is used in prayer by all the Christians in the world, up to the present day.

The entire Lord's Prayer (it is also called that, because the Lord Jesus himself taught it) is contained in the first word, "Father!" * We have the impression that this was indeed the heart of Jesus' prayer. In his mother tongue, he said "Abba", the trusting, childlike "Dad". Hence, trust is the basic tenor of the prayer he has given us.

What ought we to ask for? Should we ask God for things at all? Yes, but first of all for the most important thing: "Your kingdom come", that you should take first place and thereby set everything in our lives in its rightful place; and then, that we should have what we need: our daily bread; God's forgiveness, and forgiveness for each other, and being kept from going astray. So simple and so clear. Praying from our heart, every day, "Our Father"—that will grant us trust in God and set our lives in order.

* In German, the Lord's Prayer begins with the word "Father": *Vater unser . . .*

Eighteenth Sunday in Ordinary Time

The Gospel of Luke 12:13–21

One of the multitude said to him, "Teacher, bid my brother divide the inheritance with me." But he said to him, "Man, who made me a judge or divider over you?" And he said to them, "Take heed, and beware of all covetousness; for a man's life does not consist in the abundance of his possessions." And he told them a parable, saying, "The land of a rich man brought forth plentifully; and he thought to himself, 'What shall I do, for I have nowhere to store my crops?' And he said, 'I will do this: I will pull down my barns, and build larger ones; and there I will store all my grain and my goods. And I will say to my soul, Soul, you have ample goods laid up for many years; take your ease, eat, drink, be merry.' But God said to him, 'Fool! This night your soul is required of you; and the things you have prepared, whose will they be?' So is he who lays up treasure for himself, and is not rich toward God."

You Fool!

Quarrels over inheritances are among the most bitter there can be between relations. Families may be torn apart, even destroyed; relationships may be poisoned for many years. Why will Jesus not help there? After all, he could act as intermediary between the two brothers who were quarreling over their inheritance. Did he not say himself, "Blessed are the peacemakers" (Mt 5:9)?

It is not because he wants a comfortable life that he refuses to get involved in the brothers' dispute. He knew very well how to straighten out quarrels—for instance, when his disciples were arguing as to which of them was the greatest (something that men still love to talk about, right to this day).

Fundamentally, Jesus is offering a solution to the conflict, even in today's Gospel reading. A dispute can equally well be settled through both parties' realizing how senseless and ridiculous their behavior is. "Fool!" is how Jesus refers to the big farmer, who thinks only in terms of rates of growth and increase of yield and thus forgets the most important thing, that despite all our success and our wealth we do not dispose of our lives: "This night your soul is required of you."

Is Jesus condemning economic success? Is justice in dealing with material goods unimportant to him? Many people nurse a suspicion that the Church (and maybe Jesus himself) finds fault with all profit and worldly prosperity. People involved in economic activity like to reproach the Church with being somewhat "to the left" in economic matters.

In fact, Jesus said a good deal about good and successful business activity. The best-known example is his parable of the talents. One man has been given five talents (a talent is a very large sum of gold), and another two talents. Both of them are praised for having succeeded in doubling this capital (Mt 25:14–30). Jesus also liked to use other images from economic life: the building trade, vine growing, cattle breeding, and land agency, to mention only a few. He always gave praise whenever someone did their work well.

Even in today's parable, he does not reproach the farmer for having a good harvest. Nor does he criticize him for building new barns for the "superharvest". What he presents as idiotic foolishness is the naïve confidence of the newly rich man. He behaves as though, by attaining material wealth, he had done everything. "Economically safe on all sides: what can happen to me?"

Would we not immediately settle pointless and expensive inheritance disputes, which generate hatred, if we were a little less foolish, and thought more about how short life is? I have made it my custom, with all plans for the future, to add straightaway, "If God wills!" What do I know about what will happen tomorrow? "Beware of every kind of covetousness", says Jesus. It is stupid and dangerous!

Nineteenth Sunday in Ordinary Time

The Gospel of Luke 12:32–48

"Fear not, little flock, for it is your Father's good pleasure to give you the kingdom. Sell your possessions, and give alms; provide yourselves with purses that do not grow old, with a treasure in the heavens that does not fail, where no thief approaches and no moth destroys. For where your treasure is, there will your heart be also.

"Let your loins be girded and your lamps burning, and be like men who are waiting for their master to come home from the marriage feast, so that they may open to him at once when he comes and knocks. Blessed are those servants whom the master finds awake when he comes; truly, I say to you, he will put on his apron and have them sit at table, and he will come and serve them. If he comes in the second watch, or in the third, and finds them so, blessed are those servants! But know this, that if the householder had known at what hour the thief was coming, he would have been awake and would not have left his house to be broken into. You also must be ready; for the Son of man is coming at an hour you do not expect."

Peter said, "Lord, are you telling this parable for us or for all?" And the Lord said, "Who then is the faithful and wise steward, whom his master will set over his household, to give them their portion of food at the proper time? Blessed is that servant whom his master when he comes will find so doing. Truly I tell you, he will set him over all his possessions. But if that servant says to himself, 'My master is delayed in coming,' and begins to beat the menservants and the maidservants, and to eat and drink and get drunk, the master of that servant will come on a day when he does not expect him and at an hour he does not know, and will punish him, and put him with the unfaithful. And that servant who knew his master's will, but did not make ready or act according to his will, shall receive a severe beating. But he who did not know, and did what deserved a beating, shall receive a light beating. Every one to whom much is given, of him will much be required; and of him to whom men commit much they will demand the more."

The Treasure and the Heart

Does the Gospel speak to all men, or merely to a little troop of "chosen ones"? This is the question Peter puts to Jesus today. And it is understandable. For it can hardly be true for all men that they are to sell their belongings and give to the poor the money they raise. To whom should they sell their property, if everyone were to do it? We admire Saint Francis of Assisi (d. 1226), who did that, and maybe Saint Dominic (d. 1221), his friend, the founder of the Dominican order. Such people may be admired, but the path they take cannot be the path for everyone.

Is the Gospel for the "little flock", then, for an elite of especially pious and saintly people? Jesus gives no direct reply to Peter's question. It is as if he meant to say to him, "Do not worry about the question of how many people the Gospel applies to. You listen to what I say, and ask yourself whether that strikes home for you, whether that applies to you personally."

Not everyone is called to sell everything, like Francis and

Dominic, so as to follow Jesus in complete poverty. Yet does not Jesus' critical question hold good for me personally? "Where is your treasure? Where are the values that are decisive in your life? On the stock exchange, where, even tomorrow, shares may have dropped like a stone? In your health, which is something extremely precious but does not last forever?"

"Lay up for yourselves treasure in heaven" [Mt 6:20]! That is a saying no one can ignore. I cannot leave the response to anyone else. How much is set down under "heaven", in the accounts of my life? That is the only thing I can take with me at the final reckoning. What will I have to show before God?

What follows from this simple question? What steps do I have to take to accumulate treasure in the right place, where no moths can consume it, nor thieves steal it away? As is the case so often, Jesus replies with a parable—more precisely, with two parables, which cast light on the same point. He talks about the house servants waiting for their master's return by night and about a steward whose master comes back unexpectedly. How will he find his servants—asleep, or on the watch? How will he find the steward—taking care of the household, or careless and thinking only of his own advantage and his own pleasure?

The two parables have this point in common: we are not masters in the houses of our earthly lives. We are stewards, not owners. Life has been entrusted to us; it is not our property. The good steward never needs to fear the arrival of the "boss". If we look upon our life as a task, a gift to us, from God, then we have no need to fear even the day of doom.

Is the Gospel valid only for a "little flock", or for all men? Does Jesus not intend that as many people as possible—indeed, everyone—should be members of his flock? There is no doubt that he does! Not everyone is called, like Dominic, to leave everything behind. But we are all called to let go of everything, not to want to cling to anything anxiously. Sometime or other, we all have to leave it all. If we have been good stewards, we will not fear that hour. For our hearts will long since have found the true and lasting treasure.

Twentieth Sunday in Ordinary Time

The Gospel of Luke 12:49–53

"I came to cast fire upon the earth; and would that it were already kindled! I have a baptism to be baptized with; and how I am constrained until it is accomplished! Do you think that I have come to give peace on earth? No, I tell you, but rather division; for henceforth in one house there will be five divided, three against two and two against three; they will be divided, father against son and son against father, mother against daughter and daughter against her mother, mother-in-law against her daughter-in-law and daughter-in-law against her mother-in-law."

Not with Fire and Sword

What mysterious and terrifying words: "I came to cast fire upon the earth. . . . Do you think that I have come to give peace on earth? No, I tell you, but rather division".

Are we deceiving ourselves, then, when we picture Jesus as being above all gentle and loving, the bringer of peace? Are those critics not right after all who assert that religions bring nothing but conflict on earth? Does history justify those who reproach Christianity for its "graceless consequences" (C. Amery)? It has brought fire: the stakes at which Jews and heretics were burned. It has brought division: the wars of religion throughout Europe. And where divisions do not (any longer) lead to war, there still remain the shameful ruptures within Christendom, the many denominations that have still not regained their unity.

Many people go further and say that not only has Christianity brought fire and division but all religions have: this is because the supporters of all religions tend (they say) toward fanaticism, fundamentalism, and the use of violence. So, are religions the great disturbers of peace in the history of mankind? A glance at the twentieth century would have to warn us against making such judgments. It was not Christianity, or Islam, or any other religion that set off the horrors of two world wars but atheistic Communism and neo-pagan National Socialism [the Nazis]. It is still true, though, that up to this day wars are waged in the name of religion. And that is bad enough.

But what is Jesus really saying? The fire he is talking about is not the fire of war and devastation but the fire of the Holy Spirit. "Kindle in us the fire of your love", it says in one collect. How Jesus longs for that fire to burn. This is not the fire of the stake, for burning opponents of the faith. It is the fire of Jesus' Spirit, which is to burn away hatred in us and kindle love. People who are burning with this fire of Jesus will try to kindle other people with it.

Jesus did this without any sword. For his own part, he expressly rejected the sword. He is talking about a baptism, for which he is longing. This is the "baptism of fire" of love for one's enemies, a love that is prepared to go right to the Cross. The fire of love spreads from the Cross. "Love until it hurts", Mother Teresa (d. 1997) used to say.

And why is there division? Because we have to decide: for or against Christ, for or against love. That can bring divisions, even within a family, when one person decides in favor of Jesus and the Church, and another against. That may lead to painful ruptures, to mockery, misunderstanding, and mutual recrimination.

And what should one do if it comes to that? Make efforts to love, for love alone can construct bridges of understanding; and never forget that the division usually runs through one's own heart, too. (I am myself often divided between love of Christ, of what is good, and my weaknesses, which incline me toward evil.) Anyone who knows this will be more patient, and more loving, with others.

Twenty-first Sunday in Ordinary Time

The Gospel of Luke 13:22–30

[Jesus] went on his way through towns and villages, teaching, and journeying toward Jerusalem. And some one said to him, "Lord, will those who are saved be few?" And he said to them, "Strive to enter by the narrow door; for many, I tell you, will seek to enter and will not be able. When once the householder has risen up and shut the door, you will begin to stand outside and to knock at the door, saying, 'Lord, open to us.' He will answer you, 'I do not know where you come from.' Then you will begin to say, 'We ate and drank in your presence, and you taught in our streets.' But he will say, 'I tell you, I do not know where you come from; depart from me, all you workers of iniquity!' There you will weep and gnash your teeth, when you see Abraham and Isaac and Jacob and all the prophets in the kingdom of God and you yourselves thrust out. And men will come from east and west, and from north and south, and sit at table in the kingdom of God. And behold, some are last who will be first, and some are first who will be last."

The Narrow Door

Was that a theoretical question, "Will those who are saved be few?" Was the person who asked trying to get some kind of statistic from Jesus? Such a percentage of people will get to heaven, and the rest will go to hell? What was that person interested in when he approached Jesus with that question? We can at any rate credit him with being concerned with the question of what happens after death. That was not all the same for him, and he knew that it is not a matter of course for us to get to heaven—that is, to be saved eternally and not to be forever lost.

People in earlier centuries were profoundly concerned by the question of eternal salvation. Has the interest in the subject faded today? Even we cannot totally ignore this question. At the end of life, when we are growing old, the question becomes inescapable: "What have I done with my life? What is awaiting me after death?"

As is the case so often, Jesus makes no direct reply to the question put to him. What is decisive is not whether you know, in theory, whether many people will get to heaven or just a few. It is far more important that you do what you can to reach the goal yourself. You yourself have to "strive to enter by the narrow door".

So it is a narrow door through which I have to pass. This is no path for a pleasant stroll, nor is it a wide road, by which I get to heaven. Are there only a few people who manage it, then, after all? Jesus avoids giving numbers. He is addressing me, personally. The question is not how many others will find their way through the narrow door. You yourself have to stake everything on your life reaching its goal.

Where is this narrow door? Not simply at the end of my life, when I have to pass through the "needle's eye" of the hour of my death. The narrow door stands in the middle of my life. I can always pass it by, or go through it. Every little gesture of attention, every kind word, every step in exercising my willpower, so as not to give way to my desires and moods but turn toward someone who needs me, is itself a step through the narrow door. Every time I do not hit back when I receive an undeserved blow, every time I assent to a cross I have to bear is itself taking me part of the way through the little door that leads to the blessed life.

And, as is so often the case, Jesus makes clear what he means through a parable. If you do not start to work on yourself until the hour of your death (and that may arrive quite suddenly), it is too late. Then Jesus says, "I do not know you" [Mt 25:12]. It is a matter of choosing the narrow door here and now, instead of the broad path of comfort and selfishness.

And what if I realize, with horror, that up to now I have far too often chosen the broad path? It is not too late to wake up. I am still able to do good, even if in only very little things. Jesus will see them, and with great patience and love he will help me through the narrow door!

Twenty-second Sunday in Ordinary Time

The Gospel of Luke 14:1, 7–14

One sabbath when [Jesus] went to dine at the house of a ruler who belonged to the Pharisees, they were watching him. . . .

Now he told a parable to those who were invited, when he marked how they chose the places of honor, saying to them, "When you are invited by any one to a marriage feast, do not sit down in a place of honor, lest a more eminent man than you be invited by him; and he who invited you both will come and say to you, 'Give place to this man,' and then you will begin with shame to take the lowest place. But when you are invited, go and sit in the lowest place, so that when your host comes he may say to you, 'Friend, go up higher'; then you will be honored in the presence of all who sit at table with you. For every one who exalts himself will be humbled, and he who humbles himself will be exalted."

He said also to the man who had invited him, "When you give a dinner or a banquet, do not invite your friends or your brothers or your kinsmen or rich neighbors, lest they also invite you in return, and you be repaid. But when you give a feast, invite the poor, the maimed, the lame, the blind, and you will be blessed, because they cannot repay you. You will be repaid at the resurrection of the just."

People were watching him carefully. It was not from goodwill that they were watching. People mistrusted him and were wanting to find some good reason for their own mistrust. Was Jesus really pious? Did he strictly keep God's commandments, especially the holy sabbath rest? Was he not, rather, a revolutionary? The more Jesus did good, the more critical the people watching him became. Was he not too good, too tolerant? He sits down at the table not just with pious Pharisees but also with public sinners—with the tax collectors and prostitutes. And he says, quite openly, "It is the sick who need a physician; I have come for sinners—they need healing" [see Lk 5:31–32].

Jesus, too, is watching carefully—but in a different way from those who want to find confirmation for their negative prejudices. It is as a doctor of the soul that Jesus sees people. He sees with unremitting clarity our weaknesses and mistakes. He immediately sees through the daily games of vanity and pompousness. Everyone is pushing and shoving his way to the front, to the places of honor at the banquet. Am I blushing at the memory of how, now and then, I have acted with equal vanity?

Is Jesus' good advice not simply another clever dodge? "Choose a low place at the banquet, and then perhaps you will be invited to come up higher, in front of everybody: 'Friend, go up higher!'" This is not a clever dodge but a test. If I choose the lowest place and am overlooked on that account and get stuck down there, ignored by the guests of honor, what then? Am I angry, annoyed, or bitter about it? Or have I honestly chosen a low place? Everyone will be able to see by my face the result of the test. Have I truly understood in my heart that what matters is how I stand before God and not whether other people assign me a place of honor?

It is at this point that Jesus' observation acquires its full depth and weight of meaning. The banquet is a reflection, an anticipation, of the heavenly feast. Whenever Jesus talks about heaven, he likes to use the image of a wedding feast. How we shall be astonished when—let us hope!—we all one day get to take part in the heavenly banquet. Who will take the places of honor there? Not those who have constantly made their way forward here on earth; only those who are great in God's eyes will be sitting up there. Perhaps it will be precisely those who were regarded as "of little account" by other people but who had a great heart.

That accounts for Jesus' second observation: There is so much calculation among you! "You invited me, so I will invite you." No, you should invite the very people who cannot give you anything in return. That is exactly what God does with you! What have you to offer him? Nevertheless, he invites you as his guest every Sunday. Do it the way he does!

Twenty-third Sunday in Ordinary Time

The Gospel of Luke 14:25–33

Now great multitudes accompanied [Jesus]; and he turned and said to them, "If any one comes to me and does not hate his own father and mother and wife and children and brothers and sisters, yes, and even his own life, he cannot be my disciple. Whoever does not bear his own cross and come after me, cannot be my disciple. For which of you, desiring to build a tower, does not first sit down and count the cost, whether he has enough to complete it? Otherwise, when he has laid a foundation, and is not able to finish, all who see it begin to mock him, saying, 'This man began to build, and was not able to finish.' Or what king, going to encounter another king in war, will not sit down first and take counsel whether he is able with ten thousand to meet him who comes against him with twenty thousand? And if not, while the other is yet a great way off, he sends an embassy and asks terms of peace. So therefore, whoever of you does not renounce all that he has cannot be my disciple."

Neglecting Everything

Can we both love and hate at the same time? Loving and honoring our parents—that is what the fourth commandment enjoins. Loving our wives and children is what human nature itself teaches us, and certainly our faith teaches this, too. Hatred and strife between brothers and sisters is certainly not what corresponds to God's will. And besides that, it is much nicer and much more pleasant when brothers and sisters like each other.

And yet Jesus tells us we have to "hate" all these—father, mother, wife and children, brothers and sisters—if we want to be his disciples. "Hate" is what is written in the text of the Gospel and not "think little of", the toned-down version that our contemporary Bible translation makes of it, obviously not wanting to horrify the readers' eyes or the ears of those who hear it. Yet if "hate" is unambiguously there in the Gospel, then that can be only the genuine expression of Jesus, which Luke the Gospel writer has allowed to stand because it does indeed come from Jesus.

Jesus—preaching hatred, the way some people do even today? That certainly cannot be it, given that he himself, after all, taught, "Love your enemies! Do good to those who hate you!" [see Lk 6:27]. If we are to love our enemies, then certainly all the more our own family.

What is Jesus trying to say? Perhaps one little saying will help us here: we are supposed to "hate" even our own lives (literally, *soul* [Vulgate: *animam*, Greek *yuchn*]). It is now becoming quite incomprehensible. Does not God's holiest commandment say, "Love your neighbor as yourself"? How can I possibly love my neighbor if I despise myself, if I cannot bear myself, if, indeed, I hate myself?

By now it has certainly become clear that, with the shocking word "hate", Jesus is not preaching hatred but trying to wake us up. We are supposed to love our families but not to make a god, an idol, out of them. God comes before even our own families, before our parents, our spouses, our children—indeed, he comes before me myself. I am not the ultimate standard, and the wishes and interests of the family are not the highest values there are.

I experience this truth, painfully, time and again: There is a young man, or a young woman, with a clear call to put God in first place and to become a priest or to join a religious order. Yet the parents fight against this with all their might, bring pressure to bear, reject their child, and do everything to to turn the young person away from this vocation—as if it would be a catastrophe for the family if their son or daughter chose a spiritual calling.

In marriage, and even in friendship, there is time and again a drama, where one spouse or friend becomes jealous of the other because God has taken first place in the other's life. Jesus speaks quite energetically here. Even the best marriage or friendship is no substitute for God, who should always take first place. Anyone who tries to live this out finds that God is not in competition with the spouse or friend and takes nothing away from the relationship.

It can sometimes take a very long time, however, before the other person discovers and realizes this truth. For the person who is trying to follow Jesus, that situation may become a real cross. I know parents who rejected their daughter because she went into a convent, and I know married persons who have to suffer a great deal for their faith—from their own spouses, whom they love. Perhaps that is why Jesus uses such a harsh word here.

Twenty-fourth Sunday in Ordinary Time

The Gospel of Luke 15:1–10

Now the tax collectors and sinners were all drawing near to hear [Jesus]. And the Pharisees and the scribes murmured, saying, "This man receives sinners and eats with them."

So he told them this parable: "What man of you, having a hundred sheep, if he has lost one of them, does not leave the ninety-nine in the wilderness, and go after the one which is lost, until he finds it? And when he has found it, he lays it on his shoulders, rejoicing. And when he comes home, he calls together his friends and his neighbors, saying to them, 'Rejoice with me, for I have found my sheep which was lost.' Just so, I tell you, there will be more joy in heaven over one sinner who repents than over ninety-nine righteous persons who need no repentance.

"Or what woman, having ten silver coins, if she loses one coin, does not light a lamp and sweep the house and seek diligently until she finds it? And when she has found it, she calls together her friends and neighbors, saying, 'Rejoice with me, for I have found the coin which I had lost.' Just so, I tell you, there is joy before the angels of God over one sinner who repents."

Joy That Is Contagious

This "all" at the beginning is astonishing. Is Luke—the Evangelist who is so careful about details—exaggerating when he says that "all" the tax collectors and sinners were drawing near to Jesus at that time, to listen to him? Certainly it must have made people wonder, that the very people who were despised by the "righteous" were the ones who felt drawn toward Jesus. And there must have been many of them—the many marginal people in situations of difficulty, people whose lives were not "in order", those who could not cope with life. What attracted them to Jesus? Why was it they in particular who wanted to hear him, while the "pious" people got worked up about the way that Jesus was getting involved with such people, indeed, that he was eating at the same table with them? Sharing a meal, in those days, was more than keeping company with someone—it had a profound religious significance. Keeping table fellowship was the same as fellowship of faith. Breaking bread with someone meant also sharing their faith. Whenever Jesus sits down to a meal with "sinners", he is saying to them, "God has forgiven you; he accepts you, you are reconciled to him."

Jesus replies to his critics with the two parables of the lost sheep and of the lost coin—but especially with the parable that follows them, that of the prodigal son.

In this connection I am always reminded of our parish priest when I was young—he was someone we all truly loved. He was loving kindness in person. Many pious people thought he was too good and that he went too far. The way he visited even the people who frequented nightclubs and had a bad reputation, the way he did not pass by the doors of those people who had a questionable lifestyle—that made a big impression on me as a youth. When he died very suddenly, still quite young (he was fifty-four), everyone mourned him deeply.

What was his secret? What is the secret of Jesus? The parable says it: he is not indifferent to anyone. Like the shepherd, he goes after the lost sheep until he can find it and bring it home. Even though the little lost coin is not worth very much, the housewife searches for it until she finds it.

Yet is it not too great a risk, leaving the ninety-nine other sheep just on account of the one? Is this a measured, appropriate response? Are the ninety-nine not far more important than the one, which has perhaps gotten lost through its own fault? If it had paid more attention, it would not have taken the wrong path. Why should the others suffer on account of the one that has gotten lost?

Jesus is not mocking when he says that ninety-nine righteous people do not need to repent. It is fine and good and very pleasing to be on the right road, and Jesus is certainly not criticizing those who are honestly pious and straightforward. But he wants the "pious" people to rejoice over each person who "finds his way". No words are strong enough to express this: there is more rejoicing in heaven among the angels—God himself rejoices more—over one person who finds his way back to God than over all the others who do not need to turn around and find their way back. When I hear about this joy, then I always have to recall the radiantly joyful face of our parish priest back home; and his joy was simply catching.

Twenty-fifth Sunday in Ordinary Time

The Gospel of Luke 16:1–13

[*Jesus*] *also said to the disciples, "There was a rich man who had a steward, and charges were brought to him that this man was wasting his goods. And he called him and said to him, 'What is this that I hear about you? Turn in the account of your stewardship, for you can no longer be steward.' And the steward said to himself, 'What shall I do, since my master is taking the stewardship away from me? I am not strong enough to dig, and I am ashamed to beg. I have decided what to do, so that people may receive me into their houses when I am put out of the stewardship.' So, summoning his master's debtors one by one, he said to the first, 'How much do you owe my master?' He said, 'A hundred measures of oil.' And he said to him, 'Take your bill, and sit down quickly and write fifty.' Then he said to another, 'And how much do you owe?' He said, 'A hundred measures of wheat.' He said to him, 'Take your bill, and write eighty.' The master commended the dishonest steward for his prudence; for the sons of this world are wiser in their own generation than the sons of light. And I tell you, make friends for yourselves by means of unrighteous mammon, so that when it fails they may receive you into the eternal habitations.*

"He who is faithful in a very little is faithful also in much; and he who is dishonest in a very little is dishonest also in much. If then you have not been faithful in the unrighteous mammon, who will entrust to you the true riches? And if you have not been faithful in that which is

another's, who will give you that which is your own? No servant can serve two masters; for either he will hate the one and love the other, or he will be devoted to the one and despise the other. You cannot serve God and mammon."

God and Mammon

We have to serve someone or something, whichever way you look at it. That is the reasonable statement of Jesus in today's Gospel reading. "You cannot serve God and mammon." Literally translated, "serve" means "be the slave of". Being a slave of mammon—there is certainly some danger of that. The rich man believes that money sets him free. In reality, it dominates him. Here, Jesus is addressing something that has often been observed: money rules the world. "How much does it make?" "How can profits be increased?" "How can share prices be raised?" Those are the questions that dominate the world. And nothing seems to change in that respect, in spite of all the pious declarations. It is difficult to believe that international politics are first and foremost about great ideals and not about hard-as-nails economic interests. And if one looks closer, then one cannot be rid of the impression that the "great people of the world" are more the unfree slaves of those interests than the people who are freely shaping them. These people are all constantly being driven by so-called practical constraints imposed on them by the economic forces.

The "little people of the world", however, are still less free. They are forced by necessity to struggle daily for their survival. More and more people, even among us, in the European welfare fortress, have to look at every euro twice before they spend it. The cares of tomorrow are becoming the oppressive burden of every today. It looks as though none of us can get enough: some because they want even more, although they have far more, by a long shot, than they really need in life; others, because they cannot even get enough of what they most need.

Yet have we any free choice about finding a different lord for ourselves than mammon? Who can escape from the dominance of money? Jesus does indeed challenge us in decided fashion to set ourselves free from slavery to the god mammon. And there is only one way to do that, as he tells us unequivocally: Become a servant of God! Only then will you be free. He is the only lord who will not reduce you to slavery. If you serve him, then you are neither the slave of money nor the slave of your own passions.

Perhaps my affliction at being so unfree has in the meantime become great enough for me to yearn to be free. Yet how can I manage that? How can I get out of the "material constraints" and out of the straitjacket of my greed?

On this point, Jesus recounts an astonishing parable. How smart, how clever the "sons of this world" are, after all! They know all about making friends with money (which is usually not theirs at all). Do as they do! You should not become a swindler like this unjust steward. But whenever you have more than you absolutely need, then be generous, be ready to help, and think of those who are in need. That way, you are showing you are not the greedy slave of your money. It is true that money rules the world. Yet there is also the world power of love of one's neighbor. Worldwide, there is an infinite amount of good being done, daily and hourly. And this major power of goodness and solidarity is the great hope of all those who are unwilling sufferers beneath the servitude of mammon. As long as this power exists, the world is not lost.

There is a second thing Jesus shows us, about how we can

get free from the slavery of mammon: by being true and reliable in small things. Cheating, corruption, abuse, and poor administration likewise begin with small things. They often end in disasters. Thank God that those are still the exceptions. Thank God that even in dealing with money, people act very carefully, correctly, and reliably. These things are a prerequisite for a country not to decline into chaos and injustice. Woe to the country whose sole god is mammon. Mammon is not a good ruler.

Twenty-sixth Sunday in Ordinary Time

The Gospel of Luke 16:19–31

[Jesus said,] "There was a rich man, who was clothed in purple and fine linen and who feasted sumptuously every day. And at his gate lay a poor man named Lazarus, full of sores, who desired to be fed with what fell from the rich man's table; moreover the dogs came and licked his sores. The poor man died and was carried by the angels to Abraham's bosom. The rich man also died and was buried; and in Hades, being in torment, he lifted up his eyes, and saw Abraham far off and Lazarus in his bosom. And he called out, 'Father Abraham, have mercy upon me, and send Lazarus to dip the end of his finger in water and cool my tongue; for I am in anguish in this flame.' But Abraham said, 'Son, remember that you in your lifetime received your good things, and Lazarus in like manner evil things; but now he is comforted here, and you are in anguish. And besides all this, between us and you a great chasm has been fixed, in order that those who would pass from here to you may not be able, and none may cross from there to us.' And he said, 'Then I beg you, father, to send him to my father's house, for I have five brothers, so that he may warn them, lest they also come into this place of torment.' But Abraham said, 'They have Moses and the prophets; let them hear them.' And he said, 'No, father Abraham; but if some one goes to them from the dead, they will repent.' He said to him, 'If they do not hear Moses and the prophets, neither will they be convinced if some one should rise from the dead.' "

The Poor Man as a Bridge

This is a shocking story. Let us not be in too much of a hurry to say that it is "only" a parable, a made-up story. It is, unfortunately, a picture drawn from life by someone who knows, as no one else does, what happens in people's lives, and especially in their hearts.

In our world of today, the "Lazaruses" lying before the doors of the rich people are innumerable. In many countries, it is literally the way it was even in Jesus' time: they lie there, weak and "full of sores", hungry—starving—and also there is no lack of dogs roaming about amid their misery and squalor.

In our country, they do not lie on the streets. Our various deprivations are less visible yet just as much "in front of our door": loneliness, spiritual need, and increasingly also material need.

Behind his door lives "a rich man". Jesus does not give him a name. Things are going well for him, and he enjoys having things go well. Does Jesus begrudge him his wealth? Is Jesus a social revolutionary who is stirring things up against rich people? That is not the theme of this story. It concerns something far, far worse: the rich man no longer sees the poor man in front of his door. Perhaps the rich man is not a wicked man at all. He may be generous and openhearted with his friends. Yet he has somehow become blind. That is the great danger. The failings and the omissions count most against us. What I fail to do has been irretrievably missed.

That seems to be what Jesus is trying to say with the glimpse he offers into what lies beyond death. This is not any kind of "report" on heaven and hell, on paradise and damnation. Jesus means to shake us up: now is the time to do something. After death, it is too late. Over there, there is an unbridgeable abyss between paradise, "Abraham's bosom", and "Hades", the place of torment. Once we are over there, that abyss can no longer be crossed. Yet it is possible now. You need only to open your door and become aware of Lazarus. If his want, his affliction, go to your heart, if you share your bread with him, then there is no longer any gulf between you.

In his torments in Hades, the rich man asks Abraham to send Lazarus across with a drop of water to relieve his lot. Does that not mean, in plain words, "This poor man is the bridge that can bring you over the abyss of your eternal misery; but you must step out on the bridge now, while there is still time"?

Jesus himself hints at the poor man's significance when he gives him a name: Lazarus. Before God, the poor man is not just a number, nameless. And still more clearly, in Hebrew "Lazarus" means "God comes to help." God does not merely help the poor man by vouchsafing him paradise. He helps rich people through the poor, that their hearts may not be hardened.

Anyone who passes by poor people (of whatever kind) in life will perish at the end. That is Jesus' earnest and weighty message. Since Jesus' time, many people have accepted it. Many live in accordance with it without having heard it, because they quite simply do not overlook the Lazarus before their own door. He will help them eventually to reach their goal "beyond".

Twenty-seventh Sunday in Ordinary Time

The Gospel of Luke 17:5–10

The apostles said to the Lord, "Increase our faith!" And the Lord said, "If you had faith as a grain of mustard seed, you could say to this sycamine tree, 'Be rooted up, and be planted in the sea,' and it would obey you.

"Will any one of you, who has a servant plowing or keeping sheep, say to him when he has come in from the field, 'Come at once and sit down at table'? Will he not rather say to him, 'Prepare supper for me, and put on your apron and serve me, till I eat and drink; and afterward you shall eat and drink'? Does he thank the servant because he did what was commanded? So you also, when you have done all that is commanded you, say, "We are unworthy servants; we have only done what was our duty.'"

Increase Our Faith!

Unfortunately, the Church too finds herself sometimes figuring in negative headlines. What does a Christian want on days like that? It hurts us whenever mistakes and failures within the great community of the Church are worked to death in public. It shames us that sins and wrongdoing are found among Christian people. There will always be such things because Christians are human and are therefore sinners.

There is a great temptation to wish for one thing above all: peace and quiet once more—a justifiable wish but inadequate. Whenever mistakes and wrongdoing are denounced, that hurts us, and it is often associated with hypocrisy. ("Let him who is without sin cast the first stone", said Jesus [see Jn 8:7].) Yet this is also a process of purifying, which can in the end be good and healthy.

That is why I am impressed by what the Apostles ask of Jesus in today's Gospel reading. They ask not that people should say nice things about them; not that they should "make it"—succeed by human standards; but they ask just one thing, "Increase our faith!"

They are asking for the thing that is really the most important: a profound and solid faith. That means a strong and unshakable trust in God. And that, in turn, means building all their hopes on God's holding everything in his kind hands—even when there is a tempest, when a strong contrary wind is blowing in your face, when—from a human point of view—everything is tottering.

People come to mind in whom I have found just such a strong faith. They provide a firm handhold for others and give them confidence. Yet what do we imagine when we talk about a "strong faith"? What were the Apostles hoping to get by their request? Jesus' reply gives us food for thought: "If you had faith as a grain of mustard seed. . . ." The mustard seed is absolutely tiny. So Jesus is saying, "Even a very small amount of faith can work great things—such as transplanting a tree, with its deep roots, into the sea: that is, something quite impossible!" Is that right? Yes, quite certainly, if you understand faith properly. "Faith" means simply trusting in God. Even if your trust in God is as small as a mustard seed it is nonetheless strong and effective when it means trusting in God and not just in your own strength.

You think you just will not be able to manage it—solving a problem or clearing some difficulty. In this case, "faith" means trusting that God can help you nevertheless, that he will do things the way he knows how and the way he chooses.

Jesus expounds that in a somewhat acerbic parable. The servant has first of all to deal with all his tasks, and only then can he himself rest. He is not deserving of any particular thanks if he has merely performed his duty and done what he is supposed to do. Do your part, and then God will do his. Saint Ignatius of Loyola (d. 1556) puts it like this: "Act as if everything depended on you, and pray as if everything depended on God." Having faith does not mean taking it easy and letting everything take its course. I have to do what I can, but God will grant what is decisive. Strengthen my trust in that!

Twenty-eighth Sunday in Ordinary Time

The Gospel of Luke 17:11–19

On the way to Jerusalem [Jesus] was passing along between Samaria and Galilee. And as he entered a village, he was met by ten lepers, who stood at a distance and lifted up their voices and said, "Jesus, Master, have mercy on us." When he saw them he said to them, "Go and show yourselves to the priests." And as they went they were cleansed. Then one of them, when he saw that he was healed, turned back, praising God with a loud voice; and he fell on his face at Jesus' feet, giving him thanks. Now he was a Samaritan. Then said Jesus, "Were not ten cleansed? Where are the nine? Was no one found to return and give praise to God except this foreigner?" And he said to him, "Rise and go your way; your faith has made you well."

Have Mercy!

There they are, to this day: the lepers. I saw them in Nigeria, sitting at the side of the road, stretching out their mutilated hands for help. You have to master your feelings just so as to look at their faces, ravaged by the disease. Today, just as it did then, in the time of Jesus, this dreadful disease arouses revulsion and dread. The lepers are, as it were, rejected. The island of Molokai, near Hawaii, used to be an island of exiles; those who had fallen victim to leprosy were shipped out there and abandoned, left to their miserable fate. A Belgian priest,

Damian de Veuster, was so shaken by what happened to them that he volunteered to go to them, bringing the message of the love of God to these people who had been, as it were, buried alive. He was active among them for many years, living out the Gospel of hope and translating it into action, until he became one of them himself in the fullest sense. He died of leprosy in 1889.

Blessed Damian de Veuster had been seized by the love of Jesus for the poorest people. Like Jesus, he did not pass them by, he did not look away from their misery; he looked into their disfigured faces and saw in them the person, the brother or sister, who was suffering.

"Have mercy on us!" This loud call for help, the lepers' cry of distress, touched Jesus to the heart. Leprosy has vanished from our society, but what has not vanished is the kind of pestilence that separates people and isolates them in their loneliness. I am thinking of the many—too many—young people who have fallen victim to drugs. And many of the long-term unemployed experience their situation like a sort of disease, on account of which many people shrink from them. They are avoided; it is painful for people to hear that they are still without work.

In those days, in the time of Jesus, leprosy was social death. The lepers were like living dead. How many people today find themselves like that: dead people moving around among the living? People who are mentally ill sometimes describe their situation in words like that.

In those days, lepers very rarely recovered. Healing of leprosy was seen as a miracle, almost as great as the raising of the dead. Are there miracles like that today? I have seen them. Anyone can see them, in the Cenacolo community, for instance, in which young drug addicts really come to a new life. There is one of these communities at Kleinfrauenheid, in the Austrian province of Burgenland. Anyone who sees the young men there, the way they work and pray and are joyful, full of life and vigor, cannot imagine that all of them were once candidates for death from drug addiction—true modern lepers.

The captivating Italian nun Elvira who founded these communities—which have now become quite numerous—tells us clearly how such miracles come about. Jesus was victorious over death: he is living and working miracles, just as much now as he did two thousand years ago—miracles that we can see and touch!

It is of course sad that only one of the ten lepers who were healed thanked Jesus. That is probably, above all, a question addressed to me personally. For has Jesus not also healed me—through his mercy, in which he accepts me and loves me? Have I forgotten that so quickly? Or have I still got to learn to grasp it?

Twenty-ninth Sunday in Ordinary Time

The Gospel of Luke 18:1–8

[At that time Jesus] told them a parable, to the effect that they ought always to pray and not lose heart. He said, "In a certain city there was a judge who neither feared God nor regarded man; and there was a widow in that city who kept coming to him and saying, 'Vindicate me against my adversary.' For a while he refused; but afterward he said to himself, 'Though I neither fear God nor regard man, yet because this widow bothers me, I will vindicate her, or she will wear me out by her continual coming.'" And the Lord said, "Hear what the unrighteous judge says. And will not God vindicate his elect, who cry to him day and night? Will he delay long over them? I tell you, he will vindicate them speedily. Nevertheless, when the Son of man comes, will he find faith on earth?"

The Very Troublesome Widow

This parable of Jesus is—as always—absolutely taken from life, life as it was in those days, just as it is today. There are two characters in the story: the judge and the widow. Where the law is properly administered, a widow in need can trust the judge to be free of corruption and to give judgment justly, and to grant her justice where she has suffered injustice. Happy the land in which the judges deliver their verdicts in accordance with justice and the law, in which corruption and arbitrary preferences are not predominant! We can see from almost every page in the Bible that such a situation does not exist as a matter of course. God was always having to remind people, through the prophets, of poor people's rights. Again and again, we are warned not to give more respect to persons than to truth and justice. The test of a good society has always been whether rich and poor, powerful people and unimportant ones, are given the same treatment before the law.

Jesus starts from the assumption that in his day it was often not like that. The judge in the parable cares nothing for God or for people's need. The only things that count for him are power and his own welfare. The widow is the picture of misery that cries aloud to heaven. Who is taking any trouble about her? Who is seeing to it that she gets her rights? I shall never forget the sight of a prison in a certain country in South America: anyone who can pay will not stay there long; anyone who cannot pay bribes will stay locked up.

And is God looking at that? Why does he allow so much injustice? Why is he silent concerning the activities of this godless judge? Where is he while his people "cry to him day and night"? Where was he during the mass rapes? Where was he when people were tortured in prisons? Where is he at the point of "I cannot go on", in situations where there is no way out?

Jesus is trying to say to his audience, to us, that we "ought always to pray". And he makes it clear with this story about the widow. She does not ask quietly, as if ashamed, for what she wants; she cries aloud and makes herself a nuisance; she gives the judge no peace and harasses him, till he even feels threatened by her—he might even get a black eye from this aggressive pauper.

Should we cry to God like that? Is it permissible to wrangle with God the way Job did? To curse about him, or even at him, whenever his silence, and the way he appears to be just a spectator, make us despair?

One thing is certain: that pleases God more than if we just keep silence. God praised Job, who had unimaginable suffering to bear, for disputing with him. Yet do we dare to talk to God like that? People often say, "How can a good God allow such suffering?" Do not ask yourself that—ask God! Rattle God's door, bang at his heart, like this widow did at the judge's door. Jesus shows us how that is a prayer that will move God's heart.

God will "speedily" help us, says Jesus. But is that true? Our places of pilgrimage are full of votive plaques giving thanks to God for assistance. Is this faith, which sustained the life of our ancestors, fading away? Will Christ still find faith upon earth? Will he find it in my case? That is what we should pray for!

Thirtieth Sunday in Ordinary Time

The Gospel of Luke 18:9–14

[Jesus] also told this parable to some who trusted in themselves that they were righteous and despised others: "Two men went up into the temple to pray, one a Pharisee and the other a tax collector. The Pharisee stood and prayed thus with himself, 'God, I thank you that I am not like other men, extortioners, unjust, adulterers, or even like this tax collector. I fast twice a week, I give tithes of all that I get.' But the tax collector, standing far off, would not even lift up his eyes to heaven, but beat his breast, saying, 'God be merciful to me a sinner!' I tell you, this man went down to his house justified rather than the other; for every one who exalts himself will be humbled, but he who humbles himself will be exalted."

The Man Who Is Close and Stands Far Off

How do I stand before God? That is the question here. What people think about me may be wrong. What I think about myself may be an illusion. All that is true is how I stand before God. I cannot deceive him, and he does not deceive himself about me, and he will not deceive me.

As usual, Jesus is holding a mirror up to us: "Look into it! Dare to look at yourself the way you are and not at what you or other people think of you. Look at the mirror of this parable. In which of these two men praying do you recognize yourself?" In the Pharisee, Jesus is showing us someone who has convinced himself that he is "righteous"—that is, that he is "okay" before God and the world. Indeed, his life is exemplary, and he knows it, and cannot repeat it often enough to himself: "Thank God I am not like these other people I read about in the newspaper every day, like those criminals, who attack other people and rob them; or like those swindlers, who engage in crooked rackets until everything falls apart and lands them behind bars; or like those adulterers, who leave their wives and children high and dry and run off with someone else."

Why are we so often inclined to compare ourselves with other people? It mostly happens in the way the Pharisee does it: we look for reasons to set ourselves above other people—and find them; reasons to regard ourselves as better in comparison with them: "Thank God I am not like that!" Is there not some sort of insecurity in this need to be "better"? After all, if I am at peace with myself, then I do not need to despise others! Perhaps I am suppressing awareness of my mistakes and failures by looking down on other people.

The Pharisee in Jesus' parable simply cannot get enough of this self-justification. He carefully lists all his good deeds: "I fast twice a week", far more than is required. "I give tithes to the temple of all I get." The Church contribution in Austria is reckoned at 1.1 percent of taxable income. He gives ten times as much as that—truly an exemplary "practicing" believer.

Is he in good standing before God simply on that account? Is that not often our fundamental mistake, thinking, "If I am zealous and upright, then God will like me"? The second man does not regard himself as upright and "okay". On the contrary, he knows that he has nothing to offer God. Lots of things that are not good have accumulated in his life and his work. He makes no excuses about other people and other things, such as "society", "the circumstances", or "material constraints". He admits his own guilt. And that is why he has only one, simple request: "God be merciful to me a sinner."

How do I stand before God? Like this man "standing far off", who knows his own poverty? Or like this man standing up front, who is so greatly deceived about himself? God is close to the man standing far off. The man standing up front is a long way from God, because basically he can see only himself. Nothing is more repulsive than a piety that goes hand in hand with lovelessness and contempt for other people. God does not love me because I am "upright" but because I need his mercy.

Thirty-first Sunday in Ordinary Time

The Gospel of Luke 19:1–10

[Jesus] entered Jericho and was passing through. And there was a man named Zacchaeus; he was a chief tax collector, and rich. And he sought to see who Jesus was, but could not, on account of the crowd, because he was small of stature. So he ran on ahead and climbed up into a sycamore tree to see him, for he was to pass that way. And when Jesus came to the place, he looked up and said to him, "Zacchaeus, make haste and come down; for I must stay at your house today." So he made haste and came down, and received him joyfully. And when they saw it they all murmured, "He has gone in to be the guest of a man who is a sinner." And Zacchaeus stood and said to the Lord, "Behold, Lord, the half of my goods I give to the poor; and if I have defrauded any one of anything, I restore it fourfold." And Jesus said to him, "Today salvation has come to this house, since he also is a son of Abraham. For the Son of man came to seek and to save the lost."

What Love Can Achieve

Thank you, Luke, for recording this story of Zacchaeus! What kind of knowledge would we have of Jesus without your Gospel? You have offered us marvelous insights into his life and his heart. One of the most profound insights is this story about the tiny little rich man from Jericho. At that time, everyone was outraged by the event. Would it engender agitation, gossip, and rejection nowadays as well? I fear so.

Just imagine it: News has gotten around that the Galilean, Jesus of Nazareth, is on his way to Jerusalem and will be coming through Jericho. Crowds of people who want to see him have collected by the side of the road and are waiting for the man who many people say is the promised Messiah and Savior. One of these people cannot get a good view. He is very wealthy and very much hated—a "shark" of the first order, a chief tax collector—and besides that, he is very small in stature. The multitude of little people harassed by him take their little revenge: they will not let him through! Or does he not venture to push forward? Yet he wants to see Jesus, come what may, to see "who [Jesus] is".

In this scene, the question that interests me is, do we not—do I not—continually block people's view of Jesus? Yet in spite of that, Jesus finds his way to the heart of this outcast.

Zacchaeus does something impossible. He climbs a tree like a young lad. Never mind what people say, he wants to see Jesus. So there he is, sitting in the dense foliage of the mulberry tree * and waiting for Jesus. What happens next decides the whole course of his life. Jesus looks up, sees him, and looks him in the eyes. And for the first time in a long while, Zacchaeus meets a gaze that is without hatred or rejection and without condemnation.

How does he know me, so as to call me by name? He wants to come and visit me? Me, whom everyone fears and despises? Is it conceivable that he wants to come into my house and not into the house of one of the pious and well-respected people in town?

* The English translation renders this "sycamore tree". The word used in Greek is translated "mulberry fig", a tree unfamiliar here.—Ed.

That is how Jesus touches people's hearts: not by a threatening message but by unconditional acceptance. Because Zacchaeus had such a longing to get to know Jesus, the latter went to his house in particular, to that sinner's house. Zacchaeus was touched to the heart at being paid this attention. Jesus, by his love, has achieved what no amount of getting angry or moral lecturing could do. Zacchaeus is prepared to change his life. Other people see only the scandal of Jesus' having entered this man's house in particular. For Jesus, however, the joy at this one man's conversion counts for more. He has come for those sinners who feel and know that they need to be saved. That is what "good people" find so hard to understand!

Incidentally, Zacchaeus continues in his profession. In the future, he will certainly not be raking in so much money. He will no longer be fleecing the little people, those who are defenseless. He has made good on the injustices he has done and will try not to commit any more in the future. That is Jesus' revolution. He has changed the world, not with terror and with force, but through the power of love.

Thirty-second Sunday in Ordinary Time

The Gospel of Luke 20:27–38

There came to [Jesus] some Sadducees, those who say that there is no resurrection, and they asked him a question, saying, "Teacher, Moses wrote for us that if a man's brother dies, having a wife but no children, the man must take the wife and raise up children for his brother. Now there were seven brothers; the first took a wife, and died without children; and the second and the third took her, and likewise all seven left no children and died. Afterward the woman also died. In the resurrection, therefore, whose wife will the woman be? For the seven had her as wife."

And Jesus said to them, "The sons of this age marry and are given in marriage; but those who are accounted worthy to attain to that age and to the resurrection from the dead neither marry nor are given in marriage, for they cannot die any more, because they are equal to angels and are sons of God, being sons of the resurrection. But that the dead are raised, even Moses showed, in the passage about the bush, where he calls the Lord the God of Abraham and the God of Isaac and the God of Jacob. Now he is not God of the dead, but of the living; for all live to him."

Not God of the Dead

The question as to whether there is a life after death, and what kind of life, is among the oldest questions asked by mankind. The scholars who are looking for traces of the primeval men say that they are certainly concerned with discoveries about humans, and not with animal remains, if burial gifts are discovered. Only humans bury their dead; animals do not. Anyone who buries the dead is thereby giving expression to the belief that death is not the end of everything.

In former East Germany, dominated for decades by state atheism, many dead people are not buried nowadays but are simply "disposed of". If there is neither a God nor eternal life, then why all that bother with a funeral? To remember the departed? That is certainly one reason for having graves. But is a memorial picture not enough?

For centuries, the dignified burial of the body of the person who had died had to do with the belief that "on the last day" the dead will rise. Not only the souls of the departed live for evermore—the body, too, will one day rise again.

I suspect that a good many of our contemporaries have just as much trouble with this belief as did the Sadducees—that is, the party of the temple priests and high priests—in the time of Jesus. They liked to assemble all the possible arguments against the bodily resurrection of the dead. They are expounding one of these to Jesus today—one that is still as relevant as ever. If anyone has been married several times, then whose wife, or whose husband, will she or he be, in heaven? We can positively see the mocking faces of those who put the question. They are sure they have set Jesus a trap: how will he get out?

Jesus' reply is simple. Yet it does demand faith. Our knowledge extends only as far as the limits of earthly life. In the hereafter, things are quite different. Since we know only this life, we cannot picture for ourselves the other life. Here, we are in time, and there in eternity. Hence, here, there is everything requisite for temporal life: food, marriage, conception, birth, and the succession of generations. All of that is necessary for life on this earth to continue. In the hereafter, it is different. When there is no more death, then conception, birth, and marriage cease to be necessary. What will it be like? We have no means of comparison. Jesus says that we will have become sons and daughters of God, like Christ, who rose bodily from the tomb.

There are many questions left unanswered: How can a body rise again when it has long been rotting in the soil, has disintegrated in the sea, or has been consumed by fire? Certainly not the same way as it perished in death. Here, too, it will be quite different. We can only believe in the resurrection of the dead. It cannot be proved. Yet Jesus says something that carries more authority than scientific proof: "[God] is not God of the dead, but of the living." We are helpless and at a loss in the face of death. God is not. He is life. "All live to him", even our dead.

Thirty-third Sunday in Ordinary Time

The Gospel of Luke 21:5–19

And as some spoke of the temple, how it was adorned with noble stones and offerings, [Jesus] said, "As for these things which you see, the days will come when there shall not be left here one stone upon another that will not be thrown down." And they asked him, "Teacher, when will this be, and what will be the sign when this is about to take place?" And he said, "Take heed that you are not led astray; for many will come in my name, saying, 'I am he!' and, 'The time is at hand!' Do not go after them. And when you hear of wars and tumults, do not be terrified; for this must first take place, but the end will not be at once."

Then he said to them, "Nation will rise against nation, and kingdom against kingdom; there will be great earthquakes, and in various places famines and pestilences; and there will be terrors and great signs from heaven. But before all this they will lay their hands on you and persecute you, delivering you up to the synagogues and prisons, and you will be brought before kings and governors for my name's sake. This will be a time for you to bear testimony. Settle it therefore in your minds, not to meditate beforehand how to answer; for I will give you a mouth and wisdom, which none of your adversaries will be able to withstand or contradict. You will be delivered up even by parents and brothers and kinsmen and friends, and some of you they will put to death; you will be hated by all for my name's sake. But not a hair of your head will perish. By your endurance you will gain your lives."

The End of the World

There it stood in all its splendor, with its enormous square stone blocks: the temple in Jerusalem, rebuilt in a new glory by King Herod the Great. One could be proud of it. It gave the impression of being indestructible. We can still get some vague idea of it from the famous "wailing wall".

Just as people in those days were proud of their temple, so nowadays we are proud of our Cathedral of St. Stephen in Vienna, St. Peter's in Rome, or the other great cathedrals all over Europe. The cultural power of Christianity impresses us in these monuments of faith.

Jesus prunes away every loyalty that is too external: the temple in Jerusalem is going to perish. Not one stone will be left upon another. Jesus loved the temple, and year by year he went to Jerusalem as a pilgrim. He wanted the temple to be a house of prayer, not a market hall, and on one occasion he drove the dealers out of the temple.

Yet we should not be loyal to the temple, not set our hopes upon it. Everything can perish, and one day will. Even St. Peter's is not eternal.

An apocalyptic, end-of-the-world feeling? That is not Jesus' attitude. And he gives us no information as to what will happen when, or how. He does, however, warn us to keep sober. "Take heed!" Be on the lookout! Any number of gurus and teachers of salvation will appear and puff themselves up. There have always been those people. Today it is the "wellness" gurus who are offering salvation; in the twentieth century, it was the great ideologies.

We have to avoid both things: living carelessly and superficially from day to day, and getting into a panic about the end of the world. The believer can be sure he is safe in God's hand, even at difficult times. It is for these times that Jesus is trying to prepare his audience.

What he announces is not in fact harmless: "There will be terrors!" When? Jesus gives no dates. Even if we are not visited by earthquakes, famines, and pestilences, smaller things may occur as "the end of the world": marriages break up, death sweeps away people we love, businesses fail, jobs are lost—sheer catastrophes for those involved. How can we deal with such things so as not to go under ourselves? "Stand firm!" is Jesus' reply. Jesus will not let you fall if you trust in him.

That holds true even in the persecutions that may come. What Jesus announces reads like a description of the horrors of the Nazi era or of that of the Communists. Exactly as Jesus described it was how it went for countless thousands of Christians in the twentieth century. That could happen again today—indeed, it is happening: in the Sudan and in China. And for many Christians, even in our countries, it is a little bit like that. Jesus predicted nothing else. And he holds to his promise: his help is tangible and faithful.

FEAST OF CHRIST THE KING

The Gospel of Luke 23:35–43

The people stood by, watching; but the rulers scoffed at him, saying, "He saved others; let him save himself, if he is the Christ of God, his Chosen One!" The soldiers also mocked him, coming up and offering him vinegar, and saying, "If you are the King of the Jews, save yourself!" There was also an inscription over him, "This is the King of the Jews."

One of the criminals who were hanged railed at him, saying, "Are you not the Christ? Save yourself and us!" But the other rebuked him, saying, "Do you not fear God, since you are under the same sentence of condemnation? And we indeed justly; for we are receiving the due reward of our deeds; but this man has done nothing wrong." And he said, "Jesus, remember me when you come in your kingly power." And he said to him, "Truly, I say to you, today you will be with me in Paradise."

A King like No Other

Today, the Feast of Christ the King, is the last Sunday in the Church's year. Next Sunday, we are already in Advent, and with that comes the beginning of a new year for the Church. Luke the Evangelist has kept company with us for a whole year. At the beginning of his Gospel, we find a great promise. A messenger from God tells a very young woman from the village of Nazareth that she is going to conceive a child, a son, whom she is to call Jesus. And the promise runs like this:

> "He will be great, and will be called the Son of the
> Most High;
> and the Lord God will give to him the throne of his
> father David,
> and he will reign over the house of Jacob for ever;
> and of his kingdom there will be no end." (Lk 1:32–33)

Her child is going to be a king: it is with this expectation that Mary's pregnancy begins. Not any old king, but the great promised Prince of peace, the Redeemer-king for whom people had been hoping and longing for centuries, who would bring to the Jews—and to the whole world—peace and salvation. And she is privileged to be his mother.

It sounds like mockery when at the end of his Gospel Luke the Evangelist has to recount what became of all the great hopes from this Savior of his people. His throne has turned into the Cross, that place of torture; for company, he has two robbers, one to the right and one to the left of him. The homage he receives is the mockery of those who have set this "throne" up for him, and as the ultimate in nastiness, a notice over the head of the man who is dying in such torment states the reason for his crucifixion: "This is the King of the Jews."

And thus ends the dream of the long-expected King! No, it is not finished. With Jesus hanging here on the Cross, mocked by everyone, a total failure before the eyes of all the world, it suddenly becomes apparent that he is, after all, the longed-for Redeemer. The great people and the clever ones do not understand it, but one of the criminals beside him does. What had the criminal done? We do not know. It must have been bad, at any rate, since he says to his comrade on Jesus' left, "We have been condemned justly; we are receiving the due reward of our deeds."

And it is this criminal who has been the first to grasp this: the man who has been crucified here with us is not only innocent, but he is truly the King whose reign will have no end, even though he may now be dying a miserable death on the wood of the Cross: "Jesus, remember me when you come in your kingly power." What happened in the heart of the thief on the right for him to turn so trustingly to the man crucified along with him, as his King?

Merely what has happened countless times since then, whenever someone has turned to the crucified Jesus with the simple request, "Christ, Lord, have mercy upon me (us)!" With royal, sovereign authority, Jesus says to the criminal, "Today you will be with me in Paradise." So he is a King, after all! And no power in this world can remove or destroy what he gives: eternal life. It is worthwhile living for his kingdom—and dying for it.

Lent

and

the Easter Season

First Sunday of Lent

The Gospel of Luke 4:1–13

And Jesus, full of the Holy Spirit, returned from the Jordan, and was led by the Spirit for forty days in the wilderness, tempted by the devil. And he ate nothing in those days; and when they were ended, he was hungry. The devil said to him, "If you are the Son of God, command this stone to become bread." And Jesus answered him, "It is written, 'Man shall not live by bread alone.'" And the devil took him up, and showed him all the kingdoms of the world in a moment of time, and said to him, "To you I will give all this authority and their glory; for it has been delivered to me, and I give it to whom I will. If you, then, will worship me, it shall all be yours." And Jesus answered him, "It is written,

> *'You shall worship the Lord your God,*
> *and him only shall you serve.'"*

And he took him to Jerusalem, and set him on the pinnacle of the temple, and said to him, "If you are the Son of God, throw yourself down from here; for it is written,

> *'He will give his angels charge of you, to guard you,'*

and

> *'On their hands they will bear you up,*
> *lest you strike your foot against a stone.'"*

And Jesus answered him, "It is said, 'You shall not tempt the Lord your God.'" And when the devil had ended every temptation, he departed from him until an opportune time.

Temptation

Lent is beginning. There are forty days till Easter—exactly the length of time Jesus spent fasting in the wilderness. "And he ate nothing in those days." This was radical fasting—not for the sake of slimming, not a health diet with slimming foods, but a time to be entirely with God and for God. Nothing should stand between Jesus and God, his Father. Jesus himself intends to live out, fully and completely, what he teaches his disciples to ask for from God, "Thy will be done, on earth as in heaven."

Yet there is one person who does not want that. Many people believe that the devil does not exist. They believe that he is only a fantasy, the product of a disordered imagination. Jesus always referred to Satan quite clearly. Satan was, he said, "the father of lies", and "a murderer from the beginning" [Jn 8:44]. Elsewhere Jesus calls him, straight out, the "adversary", the "enemy" who hates man because he rejects God, who loves man.

I am increasingly surprised at how many people, on the heels of the twentieth century, still doubt that this evil power, which the Bible calls "the devil", really exists. Was Hitler's murderous hatred merely the offspring of human wickedness? When Stalin deliberately wiped out millions of Ukrainian peasants through artificially contrived famine (seventy years ago), was that merely the effect of a sick imagination? A higher power with evil intentions is playing a role here. This power also tried to get Jesus into its clutches. That was what the struggle for forty days in the wilderness was all about.

Jesus was "tempted by the devil". What does "tempting"

mean? What did it consist of for Jesus? Not in the sphere of sex—which we mostly think of when people talk about temptation—in the first instance; nor in eating and drinking, where we are so easily in danger of losing all moderation. These temptations exist—we know them, unfortunately, all too well.

The three temptations for Jesus are more radical. All three are focused on a single point: power. Jesus is, after all, God's Son. "Well then, show everyone your power—apply it full strength, and you will be one hundred percent successful! Display a powerful public miracle, and everyone will acclaim you! And then everything will be yours, all power and all the empires of the world! Throw yourself down from the highest pinnacle of the temple, in front of everyone. God's angels will catch you, and everyone will be astonished at your powers."

We do not know how these temptations operated in Jesus' heart. We do know for certain, however, that he did not give in to the allure of power. He had no intention of dazzling people with external impressions. He came not to rule but to serve. That is what God sent him for, to give his life for us men. Probably he already assented to the Cross at that time, in the wilderness. The hatred of the adversary did finally bring him to the Cross, and the people who did that were, in doing it, instruments of evil: and Jesus forgave them. He was victorious over the devil, without using power, without an army, simply through staying completely faithful to the will of God.

Temptation—what does it look like today? The devil is at work in many guises. Mostly, it is little steps that, following one after another, lead us astray. All temptations have one thing in common: they look infinitely good and promising—and they leave us feeling disappointed and empty. Only what leads to God makes us happy, even if it does require us to surmount difficulties.

Jesus withstood temptation not only for himself but also for me. In cases where I fail, he has been victorious, for me, too. I can start again with him, despite my weaknesses. And even the devil is powerless to prevent this.

Second Sunday of Lent

The Gospel of Luke 9:28b–36

[Jesus] took with him Peter and John and James, and went up on the mountain to pray. And as he was praying, the appearance of his countenance was altered, and his clothing became dazzling white. And behold, two men talked with him, Moses and Elijah, who appeared in glory and spoke of his exodus, which he was to accomplish at Jerusalem. Now Peter and those who were with him were heavy with sleep but kept awake, and they saw his glory and the two men who stood with him. And as the men were parting from him, Peter said to Jesus, "Master, it is well that we are here; let us make three booths, one for you and one for Moses and one for Elijah"—not knowing what he said. As he said this, a cloud came and overshadowed them; and they were afraid as they entered the cloud. And a voice came out of the cloud, saying, "This is my Son, my Chosen; listen to him!" And when the voice had spoken, Jesus was found alone. And they kept silence and told no one in those days anything of what they had seen.

Moments on the Mountain

Two scenes in the Gospel resemble each other greatly and yet are fundamentally different from each other. In both scenes, only three of the Apostles are with Jesus: Peter, John, and James. Both times concern a decisive moment in Jesus' life.

In both scenes, we see Jesus praying while the Apostles are sleeping. Both times, Jesus' appearance changes, though of course in opposite ways. On one occasion, on Mount Tabor, his face and his clothing become shining white. On the other, in a valley, in the Garden of Gethsemane, he is seized by deathly agony—so much so, that "his sweat became like great drops of blood falling down upon the ground" [Lk 22:44].

At the beginning of Lent, the Church invites us to come with Jesus to the stillness and solitude of the high mountain. At the end of Lent, the path leads down into the valley in which Jesus was taken prisoner, to be executed. On the mountain, the three witnesses saw the dawning of something of the divine glory of Jesus. In the valley, the same three witnesses saw Jesus in his most extreme human affliction. Later, in thinking over and retelling everything they went through with Jesus, it became clear to the three Apostles that there was a close connection between these two events. What links them together, and what distinguishes them?

What both have in common is that Jesus gives himself up entirely to the will of God. Jesus knows that some difficult moments are coming his way. He has already talked about this to the Apostles on occasion, and they were horrified. Their so well-liked and successful Master, so beloved, was one day to be rejected, persecuted, and even killed? Was Jesus, through this experience on the mountain, trying to strengthen them for the trials before them?

Certainly, they were to pluck up courage. The Transfiguration of Jesus was a wonderful experience for them. Peter wanted to stop there and build three huts on the mountain, so as to capture the marvelous moment. And yet they had to come down again from Mount Tabor with Jesus. Their journey had not yet reached its goal. The Passion, the Cross, and death were still to come. On the mountain, Jesus was trying to show them that his path was not a mistaken one but corresponded to God's will. That is why, just for a moment, they were allowed to see how glorious it is when God's will entirely fills a human heart. They were permitted a brief glimpse of the radiant glory of God in Jesus.

That was what they were to remember when Jesus was before their eyes as a prisoner, and finally as a crucified man. The happy time on Tabor was in order to help them avoid despair in the dark hours of the crucifixion and not to lose faith.

Times on Tabor are rare. Yet God does grant us them so as to give us strength for the difficult hours of suffering. Times on Tabor may be moments of profound happiness, of great joy, and, above all, of intense closeness to God. They are times filled with light, presentiments of the joy of heaven. The three Apostles who were with Jesus on Mount Tabor did not forget that time, to the end of their lives.

Third Sunday of Lent

The Gospel of Luke 13:1–9

There were some [people] present at that very time who told [Jesus] of the Galileans whose blood Pilate had mingled with their sacrifices. And he answered them, "Do you think that these Galileans were worse sinners than all the other Galileans, because they suffered thus? I tell you, No; but unless you repent you will all likewise perish. Or those eighteen upon whom the tower in Siloam fell and killed them, do you think that they were worse offenders than all the others who dwelt in Jerusalem? I tell you, No; but unless you repent you will all likewise perish."

And he told this parable: "A man had a fig tree planted in his vineyard; and he came seeking fruit on it and found none. And he said to the vinedresser, 'Behold, these three years I have come seeking fruit on this fig tree, and I find none. Cut it down; why should it use up the ground?' And he answered him, 'Let it alone, sir, this year also, till I dig about it and put on manure. And if it bears fruit next year, well and good; but if not, you can cut it down.' "

There Is Still Time!

Something horrendous has happened in Jerusalem. It sounds like something on the news today, like an attack on an Israeli bus by a Palestinian suicide bomber. Passover pilgrims from Galilee, where Jesus came from, were just at the point of making their offering in the temple. This was probably the offering of the Passover lamb. Then Roman soldiers stormed in. According to Jewish law, they could not enter the temple. At the Passover festival, however, there is great tension in Jerusalem. The holy city is filled with thousands upon thousands of pilgrims. The Roman authorities were always afraid of a rising or of terrorist attacks on the institutions of Roman government. Pontius Pilate, the Roman procurator—not otherwise particularly heroic—was well known for his bloody interventions. Taking no account of the Jews' religious feelings, he had a group of Galilean pilgrims—who seemed suspicious to him—cut down in the temple, so that their blood "mingled with their sacrifices".

People reacted with shock, horror, and rage—and very many questions. No questions about being against the Romans—that was, so to speak, self-evident. A different question concerned people, then as now: "How can God allow something like that to happen?" Unlike nowadays, however, God was not accused of anything: everyone wondered in what way these people were guilty. These Galileans who were slaughtered must surely have done something, for God to allow such a punishment to fall on them. What could their sin have been?

Jesus looks at it from the completely opposite point of view. Of course those Galileans were sinners. "But do you really believe that you are not sinners just because no accident has yet happened to you? Do not think you are safe!"

In order to make it clear, he refers to another "headline" from the news of the time. In the course of digging to construct an aqueduct, a defensive tower at the Pool of Siloah was undermined and collapsed; eighteen people were buried alive beneath it. Nowadays, we would start straightaway trying to find who was responsible in the Jerusalem planning and building regulation authorities and in the construction firm. And if someone is found who is guilty in some way, this person would be punished. In those days, a different question exercised people's minds: "What was there about the victims for God to allow this catastrophe?"

Jesus radically altered the way people looked at it then, and he would do the same today. At the news of disasters of that kind, do not ask yourself "Who is responsible?" so as to point the finger at them. Do not ask first why God allows such dreadful things to happen. Ask first about yourself. You could have been among the victims. Would you have been ready, then, to come before God's face? How would the bank account for your own life look if sudden death demanded your final reckoning?

Whenever you hear dreadful news of that sort, then just reflect on how patient God is with you. He is treating you like the vinedresser who gives the barren fig tree just one last chance, even though it has borne no fruit until now. Repent; there is still time!

Fourth Sunday of Lent

The Gospel of Luke 15:1–3, 11–32

Now the tax collectors and sinners were all drawing near to hear [Jesus]. And the Pharisees and the scribes murmured, saying, "This man receives sinners and eats with them."

So he told them this parable: . . . "There was a man who had two sons; and the younger of them said to his father, 'Father, give me the share of property that falls to me.' And he divided his living between them. Not many days later, the younger son gathered all he had and took his journey into a far country, and there he squandered his property in loose living. And when he had spent everything, a great famine arose in that country, and he began to be in want. So he went and joined himself to one of the citizens of that country, who sent him into his fields to feed swine. And he would gladly have fed on the pods that the swine ate; and no one gave him anything. But when he came to himself he said, 'How many of my father's hired servants have bread enough and to spare, but I perish here with hunger! I will arise and go to my father, and I will say to him, "Father, I have sinned against heaven and before you; I am no longer worthy to be called your son; treat me as one of your hired servants."' And he arose and came to his father. But while he was yet at a distance, his father saw him and had compassion, and ran and embraced him and kissed him. And the son said to him, 'Father, I have sinned against heaven and before you; I am no longer worthy to be called your son.' But the father said to his servants, 'Bring quickly the best robe, and put it on him; and put a ring on his hand, and shoes on his feet; and bring the fatted calf and kill it, and let us eat and make merry; for this my son was dead, and is alive again; he was lost, and is found.' And they began to make merry.

"Now his elder son was in the field; and as he came and drew near to the house, he heard music and dancing. And he called one of the servants and asked what this meant. And he said to him, 'Your brother has come, and your father has killed the fatted calf, because he has received him safe and sound.' But he was angry and refused to go in. His father came out and entreated him, but he answered his father, 'Behold, these many years I have served you, and I never disobeyed your command; yet you never gave me a kid, that I might make merry with my friends. But when this son of yours came, who has devoured your living with harlots, you killed for him the fatted calf!' And he said to him, 'Son, you are always with me, and all that is mine is yours. It was fitting to make merry and be glad, for this your brother was dead, and is alive; he was lost, and is found.' "

The Prodigal Son

Few Gospel readings are so very much "gospel", good news, as this is. Who is not moved by seeing this father, who is waiting with yearning for his son, and who sees him when he is still a long way off, when he finally comes home? No word of reproach, no "Why did you do it?" but only a simple joy over the son who has given him so much trouble and who has now come back again.

Artists have captured this moment of coming home again:

the father's moving mercy as he lays his arm protectively around his son's shoulders. It does us so much good to know that Jesus is proclaiming a God like that. Not a condemnatory judge who punishes people but a forgiving and merciful father. Many people feel—quite rightly—that, in this parable, Jesus has expressed what his message really is.

Yet if we look more closely, then it becomes clear that what lay closest to Jesus' heart was by no means so easily accepted, that it did indeed, in part, meet with strong resistance. In this parable, both sons find it difficult to grasp, and to accept, their father's kindness and love. In these two sons, Jesus has shown us how we humans behave toward God.

The younger one demands his inheritance, even though in those days that was not allowed while the father was still alive. The father gives it to him, damaging his own business thereby. Jesus is saying to us here, "God leaves us free. We can even use our freedom against God and against what is good." The inheritance has soon been blown. The younger son lands in a situation of want, for which he himself is responsible. He ekes out his existence as a swineherd (for Jews, a particularly shameful thing).

Then he remembers home. Hunger drives him back again. He thinks it over: even the simplest laborers in his father's business do better than this. He works out a speech to make to his father. Is this really remorse, or merely knowing on which side his bread is buttered? Perhaps both, as is so often the case with us when we find ourselves in trouble and are sorry for what we have done wrong. In short, the younger brother hardly cuts a splendid figure.

The elder brother's wrath is all too easy to understand. There is the younger brother, exhausting his inheritance, while the elder brother has stayed faithfully at home, working hard all the time in his father's business. Yet his younger brother has hardly reached home again when everything is forgiven and forgotten. The father is beside himself with joy and takes him back as his son. And that means, in plain words, he is also restored as an heir. If he is a son, then he gets a share of the inheritance. The elder brother, then, will at some time have to share his own portion of the inheritance with that rogue of a younger brother. And he is even expected to be glad about that!

Is the merciful God whom Jesus is talking about not, after all, unfair in the way he is kind? The younger son cannot believe, at first, that his father is taking him back again. He is too inclined to despise himself for his failure in life. The elder son cannot accept the fact that, to the father, the lost son's coming back home again is more important than any matters of inheritance: He "was dead, and is alive". Both of them have to learn to understand that God intends them to be happy—and alive. All of us have to understand that it gives God the greatest joy if we, his children, find our way home to him. And the farther away from which we are coming back, the greater his joy.

Fifth Sunday of Lent

The Gospel of John 8:1–11

Jesus went to the Mount of Olives. Early in the morning he came again to the temple; all the people came to him, and he sat down and taught them. The scribes and the Pharisees brought a woman who had been caught in adultery, and placing her in their midst they said to him, "Teacher, this woman has been caught in the act of adultery. Now in the law Moses commanded us to stone such. What do you say about her?" This they said to test him, that they might have some charge to bring against him. Jesus bent down and wrote with his finger on the ground. And as they continued to ask him, he stood up and said to them, "Let him who is without sin among you be the first to throw a stone at her." And once more he bent down and wrote with his finger on the ground. But when they heard it, they went away, one by one, beginning with the eldest, and Jesus was left alone with the woman standing before him. Jesus looked up and said to her, "Woman, where are they? Has no one condemned you?" She said, "No one, Lord." And Jesus said, "Neither do I condemn you; go, and do not sin again."

Who Throws the First Stone?

Jesus' decisive pronouncement in today's Gospel reading has become something of a proverb: "Let him who is without sin among you be the first to throw a stone at her"—at the adulteress who has been caught in the act.

This is a consoling Gospel reading yet also a challenging one. It comforts us to hear that Jesus did not condemn this woman. At the same time, it is a great challenge not to condemn anyone ourselves, not to throw a stone: "Let him who is without sin among you . . ."

But let us follow Jesus into the temple in Jerusalem early in the morning. People gather around, and Jesus teaches them. Then suddenly there is a commotion. People drag a woman in and set her before Jesus, pointing at her—and she stands there in fear for her life. She is said to have been caught in the act of adultery. The punishment for that is laid down as being stoned to death. That is what the law of Moses prescribes. What will Jesus do? If he says, "Stone her", then he can be accused of not being as merciful as he always says. If he says, "Leave her alone; let her go", then they can accuse him of not keeping the law. Then they would have yet another reason for condemning him. A real "catch-22" situation!

The way Jesus "escapes" is astoundingly simple, and right to this day it calls us all into question: What does Moses say in the law of the Old Covenant? "If a man commits adultery with the wife of his neighbor, both the adulterer and the adulteress shall be put to death" (Lev 20:10). What has happened to the man? Did these men overlook him? Did they just let him get away? Did he do any less than she did? Does the law apply less to men than to women? Is it only this woman who is a sinner?

Jesus does not say all this in just those words. He says nothing. He silently writes in the sand. What did he write? We do not know, and it has been blown away long ago. Since the accusers do not leave him in peace, he straightens up again and makes this pronouncement, which has rung out down the centuries ever since.

He does not say that adultery is harmless, merely a little deviation from the path. He lets the old law stand in all its harshness. And yet he fundamentally transforms it. It is as if Jesus said, "All right, the law commands us to stone the adulteress. Someone has to begin, someone has to start to smash her up with a heavy stone. The one who begins should be the one who is without sin himself." It is no wonder that they all go away, one after the other, beginning with the oldest ones; for nobody is without sin. And thus the woman is left standing alone with Jesus.

Alone with Jesus! Finally, alone with the one in whose heart there is no condemnation, the one who looks at me without any accusations and without rejecting me, although I am standing there before him so pathetically, with my failures and my mistakes. I often find it difficult not to condemn myself, not to despise myself. He does not do that. I cannot hear often enough those marvelous words, "Neither do I condemn you." That makes it possible for me to start over again. It gives me hope. And so I can accept as applying to me what Jesus says at the end to the adulteress: "Go, and do not sin again."

Palm Sunday

The Gospel of Luke 19:28–40

[Jesus] went on ahead, going up to Jerusalem. When he drew near to Bethphage and Bethany, at the mount that is called Olivet, he sent two of the disciples, saying, "Go into the village opposite, where on entering you will find a colt tied, on which no one has ever yet sat; untie it and bring it here. If any one asks you, 'Why are you untying it?' you shall say this, 'The Lord has need of it.'" So those who were sent went away and found it as he had told them. And as they were untying the colt, its owners said to them, "Why are you untying the colt?" And they said, "The Lord has need of it." And they brought it to Jesus, and throwing their garments on the colt they set Jesus upon it. And as he rode along, they spread their garments on the road. As he was now drawing near, at the descent of the Mount of Olives, the whole multitude of the disciples began to rejoice and praise God with a loud voice for all the mighty works that they had seen, saying, "Blessed is the King who comes in the name of the Lord! Peace in heaven and glory in the highest!" And some of the Pharisees in the multitude said to him, "Teacher, rebuke your disciples." He answered, "I tell you, if these were silent, the very stones would cry out."

Passover in Jerusalem is the greatest Jewish festival. The liberation from Egypt is celebrated, the time when the Jewish people escaped from slavery in Egypt and were marvelously saved from the threat of Pharaoh's army by passing through the Red Sea.

Year by year, to this day, Passover is celebrated as the most significant festival in the Jewish calendar. In those days, at the time of Jesus, enormous multitudes of pilgrims used to come to Jerusalem—up to a hundred thousand of them. The city was not just completely overflowing with them, but a high level of tension reigned there. For according to Jewish beliefs, Pesach (Passover) is not merely a feast in remembrance of the exodus, the saving journey out of Egypt, but it is also a feast of hope. At Passover, so many people expect that Israel will be saved once again. The Messiah is to come at the Passover and set his people free from all their troubles. Year by year, accordingly, the tension ran high in Jerusalem: would the longed-for redeemer come this year, perhaps?

Hence, the Roman garrison was at the highest state of readiness. Time and again, there were risings of the Jews against the Romans in Jerusalem at the time of the Passover, and these were cruelly and bloodily repressed. The Romans liked to execute the leaders by crucifixion, as a terrible warning.

That, then, is the background to today's Gospel reading about Jesus' entry into Jerusalem. Just one more point to help us understand: on their way to Jerusalem, the pilgrims, who often traveled on foot for days on end, particularly rejoiced at the moment when they caught their first sight of Jerusalem. That was on the Mount of Olives, to the east of Jerusalem. In the villages just before the Mount of Olives, therefore, the pilgrims used to make a halt so as to prepare for their entry into Jerusalem, just as many pilgrims do even nowadays, when they are close to their journey's end.

Jesus, too, used to prepare himself on that pilgrimage. That year, however (it may have been the year 30), he did something special. He had a donkey fetched and sat himself upon it. And when they came to the Mount of Olives, at the point where you saw Jerusalem and the splendor of the temple, the enthusiasm broke forth, and the people accompanying Jesus began to cheer him. The reason for this is clear: they believed that he was the longed-for Messiah, the Savior of his people. Now, just a few days before the feast of the Passover, he was entering Jerusalem. Now the liberation would begin. They cry out to him that he is the King of Israel, who is coming in God's name. He will bring peace, they proclaim, and that could mean only a fine new age.

How many people noticed this little crowd coming into the city with Jesus? The Roman garrison did not intervene. If it had been a very big crowd, then they would certainly have done so. A few Pharisees were concerned about it and wanted to get Jesus' disciples to be quiet: "Don't make a commotion, or the Romans will intervene yet again!" Jesus' reply has become proverbial: "If they keep silent, the very stones will speak."

Without a great deal of noise, Jesus enters his city and comes into the temple, his Father's house. Only a few people take any notice of his arrival. He comes, not with any great pomp, but modestly, riding on a donkey. It has continued to be so, up to this day. For the most part, Jesus comes into our lives in unspectacular ways.

Yet his coming brings joy and hope. Through faith, we can receive him. How many generations before us have opened the doors of their lives to Christ in faith! And everywhere, the stones of our churches and chapels and wayside shrines bear witness to the fact that here, people have welcomed Christ into their lives.

Good Friday

The Passion—the Gospel of John 19:17–30

So they took Jesus, and he went out, bearing his own cross, to the place called the place of a skull, which is called in Hebrew Golgotha. There they crucified him, and with him two others, one on either side, and Jesus between them. Pilate also wrote a title and put it on the cross; it read, "Jesus of Nazareth, the King of the Jews." Many of the Jews read this title, for the place where Jesus was crucified was near the city; and it was written in Hebrew, in Latin, and in Greek. The chief priests of the Jews then said to Pilate, "Do not write, 'The King of the Jews,' but, 'This man said, I am King of the Jews.'" Pilate answered, "What I have written I have written."

When the soldiers had crucified Jesus they took his garments and made four parts, one for each soldier; also his tunic. But the tunic was without seam, woven from top to bottom; so they said to one another, "Let us not tear it, but cast lots for it to see whose it shall be." This was to fulfill the Scripture,

> *"They parted my garments among them,*
> *and for my clothing they cast lots."*

So the soldiers did this. But standing by the cross of Jesus were his mother, and his mother's sister, Mary the wife of Clopas, and Mary Magdalene. When Jesus saw his mother, and the disciple whom he loved standing near, he said to his mother, "Woman, behold, your son!" Then he said to the disciple, "Behold, your mother!" And from that hour the disciple took her to his own home.

After this Jesus, knowing that all was now finished, said (to fulfill the scripture), "I thirst." A bowl full of vinegar stood there; so they put a sponge full of the vinegar on hyssop and held it to his mouth. When Jesus had received the vinegar, he said, "It is finished"; and he bowed his head and gave up his spirit.

—the text as a whole: John 18:1—19:42

Passion

"He went out bearing his own cross to . . . Golgotha. There they crucified him." The description could not be more spare. Not a word about the horror of what was happening—but, in those days, all those who heard this brief account knew what it meant. All too often, people saw the torments of a crucifixion; and what it meant to be scourged was common knowledge. Thus, these few words were all the more powerfully effective.

"They crucified him." In later centuries, when crucifixion was no longer used as a method of execution, people tried to imagine what Jesus' way of suffering was like. They surrounded the bare words of the Gospel with a wreath of meditations. Our fourteen stations of the Cross, as we find them in most churches, grew out of that. Here, scenes based on history are mixed with others that have not been transmitted in the Bible—for instance, the person of Veronica, who handed Jesus a cloth so that he could wipe the sweat and the blood away from his face. Likewise, the way he fell three times beneath the burden of the wooden Cross is not reported in the Gospels.

People have meditated upon the sufferings of Jesus in all

ages: the strokes of the scourging and the crown of thorns, the hours of agony hanging on the Cross until death. Many of these meditations see only Jesus' coming victory over suffering and death, showing him as already bathed in the light of the Resurrection, as for instance do the fine Romanesque portrayals of the crucifixion. Others contemplate the details of the suffering, trying to rediscover what Jesus' pains and torments felt like. Many Gothic crucifixes show the tortures of the Cross with almost unbearable realism.

The climax of this is probably the *Isenheim Altarpiece* of Matthias Grünewald (d. 1528) in Colmar. It originally stood in a hospital in which people lay with the most appalling illnesses. Many of the people looked just like the atrociously damaged body of Jesus, wrecked beyond hope.

Why did Master Grünewald portray Jesus' suffering so realistically and so horribly? The question is being raised again today: "Why portray the Passion of Jesus so bloodily?"—for instance, in Mel Gibson's movie *The Passion of the Christ* (2004); or in the novel *The Master and Margarita*, by Mikhail Bulgakov (d. 1940), which depicts how dreadfully flies torment the crucified, who are thus defenseless against the swarms of them.

There are two motives for this dwelling on the sufferings of Jesus: First, his Passion really was inconceivably horrible. Even today, we are overcome with horror that people could inflict such torments on others. Such passions are still happening today. Jesus' way of the Cross reminds us not to turn our eyes away from other people's suffering.

The second motive, though, is the shattering realization, through faith, that Jesus suffered all that on my account and for my sake! In gazing on the Crucified One of the *Isenheim Altarpiece*, people who were in agony and dying could relate their suffering to his. He himself had borne their sufferings.

Looking at the One who rose again, they could see what kind of redemption awaited them. That is why it says in the old hymn "O Sacred Head, Surrounded":

> What thou, my Lord, hast suffered,
> was all for sinners' gain;
> Mine, mine was the transgression,
> but thine the deadly pain.
> Lo, here I fall, my Savior!
> 'Tis I deserve thy place;
> Look on me with thy favor,
> vouchsafe to me thy grace.

Easter Sunday

The Gospel of John 20:1–9

Now on the first day of the week, Mary Magdalene came to the tomb early, while it was still dark, and saw that the stone had been taken away from the tomb. So she ran, and went to Simon Peter and the other disciple, the one whom Jesus loved, and said to them, "They have taken the Lord out of the tomb, and we do not know where they have laid him." Peter then came out with the other disciple, and they went toward the tomb. They both ran, but the other disciple outran Peter and reached the tomb first; and stooping to look in, he saw the linen cloths lying there, but he did not go in. Then Simon Peter came, following him, and went into the tomb; he saw the linen cloths lying, and the napkin, which had been on his head, not lying with the linen cloths but rolled up in a place by itself. Then the other disciple, who reached the tomb first, also went in, and he saw and believed; for as yet they did not know the Scripture, that he must rise from the dead.

An Encounter on Easter Morning

No human being witnessed what happened during that night. The Resurrection, the most important event in all the long history of mankind, occurred without anybody's being able to see it, describe it, or record it. Jesus was dead; he had died in torment on the Cross. They had buried him in a tomb newly hewn from the rock, near to the place of execution on Golgotha. They had sealed up the tomb with a heavy stone, which was rolled across the entrance, so that no one could desecrate the body or steal it.

Two respectable men had taken care of Jesus' dead body, had taken it down from the Cross and buried it with due reverence. It was not to the Apostles' credit that none of them, Jesus' closest colleagues, did this for him. Would they simply have left Jesus hanging? Then he would have been thrown into a mass grave. Were they so terrified, so overwhelmed by their disappointment and grief that they literally "left Jesus hanging there"? No wonder that the "institutional Church", time and again, behaves in the same reprehensible way. Later, the Apostles would be able to see how they had let Jesus down, would be sorry for it, and would be honest enough not to conceal it in the Gospel stories. We may be thankful for their honesty. This serves as a model for officials of the Church, to this day.

The Church has no need to be ashamed of Mary Magdalene. This woman, who had been a great sinner and had found her way through Jesus to a true love, behaved quite differently. She went to the tomb before dawn. She was not fearful or self-pitying; in her heart was simply a deep sorrow that her beloved Master was dead. She, indeed, had stayed beside the Cross, had not abandoned Jesus in his final agony, while all the Apostles—apart from John, who likewise saw it out to the end beside the Cross—were so frightened that they stayed in hiding.

When Mary got to the tomb, she found it open and empty. It was a tremendous shock. She told the Apostles about it, and they came running. John, the younger one, ran faster, while the more ponderous Peter followed behind; yet it was Peter who was first to enter the tomb.

Time and again, these two have been interpreted symbolically. Peter is the "institutional Church", and John the "Church of love". Love is quicker, less encumbered than any institution, which has many matters of which to take account. Yet love has respect for office and lets it take the lead. There should be no rivalry between the two, for the Church needs them both: love's enthusiasm and the order of official institutions.

The two Apostles see the linen cloths lying in the tomb and realize from the way they are lying that Jesus' body cannot have been stolen. Yet where is he? They go back home with this unanswered question.

Once more, Mary Magdalene is different. She stays. She cannot go away before her Jesus has been found. Her faithfulness and her tears are not in vain. There is a thrilling encounter with Jesus, the Risen One. He addresses her by name, and then she recognizes him. She was the first of them all to be allowed to see him, him whom death could not retain.

Since that early morning of Easter Day, innumerable people have met with Jesus. They have not necessarily seen him with their own eyes. Yet they can reaffirm it: "He is alive. He has spoken to me. I have met him."

Second Sunday of Easter (Divine Mercy Sunday)

The Gospel of John 20:19–31

On the evening of that day, the first day of the week, the doors being shut where the disciples were, for fear of the Jews, Jesus came and stood among them and said to them, "Peace be with you." When he had said this, he showed them his hands and his side. Then the disciples were glad when they saw the Lord. Jesus said to them again, "Peace be with you. As the Father has sent me, even so I send you." And when he had said this, he breathed on them, and said to them, "Receive the Holy Spirit. If you forgive the sins of any, they are forgiven; if you retain the sins of any, they are retained."

Now Thomas, one of the Twelve, called the Twin, was not with them when Jesus came. So the other disciples told him, "We have seen the Lord." But he said to them, "Unless I see in his hands the print of the nails, and place my finger in the mark of the nails, and place my hand in his side, I will not believe."

Eight days later, his disciples were again in the house, and Thomas was with them. The doors were shut, but Jesus came and stood among them, and said, "Peace be with you." Then he said to Thomas, "Put your finger here, and see my hands; and put out your hand, and place it in my side; do not be faithless, but believing." Thomas answered him, "My Lord and my God!" Jesus said to him, "You have believed because you have seen me. Blessed are those who have not seen and yet believe."

Now Jesus did many other signs in the presence of the disciples, which are not written in this book; but these are written that you may believe that Jesus is the Christ, the Son of God, and that believing you may have life in his name.

Close Enough to Touch

He had told the story often. Time and again, people had asked him, "What was it like when Jesus was dying on the Cross? What was it like when you found that he—that is, his body—was no longer in the tomb? What was it like when you saw him again for the first time—when he appeared to you?"

Again and again, John had had to tell the story, until he was an old man. Christians wanted to know what it had been like at the time. Gradually, one after the other, the other Apostles died off. They all followed their Master in suffering violent death as martyrs. The first was John's own brother, James, whom King Herod Agrippa simply had beheaded. In the end, John was the only one left, the last living eyewitness. Toward the end of the first century, well advanced in years, he died of natural causes.

At some point, he had begun to set down in writing what it had been like at the time. He could select only a little material—what seemed to him most important. He had to leave out a great deal that we, with natural curiosity, would like to have known. But he was not concerned with writing down anything of lesser importance, "sidelights", so to speak. What had stayed in his memory about Easter Day?

They had barred the doors from fear. Nevertheless, Jesus

came in: suddenly he was there in their midst. I think that John was trying to say to his fellow Christians (then and now): "Have you not experienced the same thing yourselves, time and again? When you meet together on the 'first day of the week' for worship, for the Mass, often all too few of you, a frightened bunch of people—does not Jesus come into your midst? Not, indeed, visibly, as happened with us that time in Jerusalem, but nonetheless really, so that you can feel his presence and he gives you his peace?"

John can remember quite clearly the unforgettable joy they had felt "when they saw the Lord". After those dreadful days in which Jesus had been taken prisoner, condemned, and crucified, what indescribable joy they had at the fact that he was alive, that he was with them again! And you, too, have experienced that joy, again and again, whenever Jesus lets you know, after some great pain, or some heavy trouble, that he is alive and that he is with you—that he will never leave you.

And John reminds us that since then, Jesus has never ceased to pass on to us his Spirit, in baptism and confirmation and in the many graces we receive from him in the course of our lives.

John reminds us of one person in particular: his apostolic colleague "doubting Thomas". John has met many such people since then, people who are willing to believe only in what they can see and touch. To me—as I am sometimes something of a doubting Thomas—John as an old man is trying to say, "Look, you too can touch Jesus. You can meet him. Even—and in fact especially—when paying attention to the neighbor who needs your help. Then, Jesus is 'close enough to touch'."

Third Sunday of Easter

The Gospel of John 21:1–14

After this Jesus revealed himself again to the disciples by the Sea of Tiberias; and he revealed himself in this way. Simon Peter, Thomas called the Twin, Nathanael of Cana in Galilee, the sons of Zebedee, and two others of his disciples were together. Simon Peter said to them, "I am going fishing." They said to him, "We will go with you." They went out and got into the boat; but that night they caught nothing.

Just as day was breaking, Jesus stood on the beach; yet the disciples did not know that it was Jesus. Jesus said to them, "Children, have you any fish?" They answered him, "No." He said to them, "Cast the net on the right side of the boat, and you will find some." So they cast it, and now they were not able to haul it in, for the quantity of fish. That disciple whom Jesus loved said to Peter, "It is the Lord!" When Simon Peter heard that it was the Lord, he put on his clothes, for he was stripped for work, and sprang into the sea. But the other disciples came in the boat, dragging the net full of fish, for they were not far from the land, but about a hundred yards off.

When they got out on land, they saw a charcoal fire there, with fish lying on it, and bread. Jesus said to them, "Bring some of the fish that you have just caught." So Simon Peter went aboard and hauled the net ashore, full of large fish, a hundred and fifty-three of them; and although there were so many, the net was not torn. Jesus said to them, "Come and have breakfast." Now none of the dis-

ciples dared ask him, "Who are you?" They knew it was the Lord. Jesus came and took the bread and gave it to them, and so with the fish. This was now the third time that Jesus was revealed to the disciples after he was raised from the dead.

One Hundred Fifty-three Large Fish

Life goes on. It is sometimes painful for us to discover that fact after some profound disruption in our lives, perhaps after the death of someone we love. Life has to go on, somehow or other. It asserts its rights; it draws us in and involves us. There comes a moment when everyday life resurfaces.

That kind of situation came about for the Apostles after Easter. Their beloved Master's death on the Cross had just thrown them completely; they were overcome with panic, fear, and helplessness. But then came the turnaround: they found his grave empty, and somewhat later he himself appeared. After the mourning came tremendous joy: the Lord is alive; he has risen.

Soon afterward, however, they realized that life had to go on. Jesus is indeed alive, but he is no longer in this world. He appeared to them several times, but he was no longer living with them. What should they do now? They, after all, were still in this world. He had left them behind here. He was close to them, and yet they had to take charge of their own lives.

What happened to them then is a model for us, for as Christians we believe that Christ has risen again and is alive and that he is therefore very close to us. In spite of this, he does not take away from us the trouble of seeing to our daily lives. Life has to go on.

For the Apostles, that meant that they returned to their old work. The first of them were fishermen from Galilee; that is where we find them once more. They had to make a living somehow. Seven of them were going fishing. Had they forgotten their old skills? Their new start was a complete failure. In their first night out on the lake again, they caught nothing. They were correspondingly unresponsive when an unknown man on the shore invited them to come and eat with him.

It was all the more surprising that they followed the advice of the stranger on the shore and threw their net out one more time. They had not yet realized it was Jesus giving them this advice. When they suddenly found their net brimming with fish, they began to comprehend who it was that was standing there on the shore. The especially beloved disciple, John, grasped it first: "It is the Lord!"

Here I pause for a moment. For I believe that each person who is trying to be a Christian has similar experiences in everyday life. Jesus is no longer visible among us. He does not even appear anymore, as he used to on occasion at the beginning, for the Apostles and the first disciples, up to his Ascension. Yet there are still situations in which, in the midst of the cares of everyday life, we suddenly become aware—sometimes so clearly that we could almost touch him—"It is the Lord!"

John's exclamation is accompanied by joy, powerful and intense. We can experience this joy, amid impossible and seemingly meaningless difficulties, whenever something occurs like the enormous and unexpected catch of fish. Then we are clearly aware that we have not achieved that ourselves; it has been granted us as a gift. Thus, to be aware of Christ being close to us is an experience that simply makes us happy.

There is a great deal more deserving of our attention in this final chapter of the Gospel of John. Let us at least mention the 153 large fish. Why this exact number? There have been many attempts to explain it. Here is one I have found in the writings of Saint Augustine (d. 430): add up the numbers from one to seventeen—they make 153. Seventeen is made up of ten plus seven. These, the great Saint Augustine says, are a symbol for the Old Testament (Ten Commandments) and the New (seven is the "perfect" number). The Apostles had been given in their net, so to speak, the whole fullness of God's revelation. Yet there are many other attempted interpretations of this enigmatic number. What they have in common is this: this number signifies, symbolically, the whole fullness of God, which is vouchsafed to these men.

Life goes on, certainly. Yet what is more certain is that Jesus is there, in the midst of my daily life. He is calling to me from the farther shore of eternity. He is helping me, giving signs of his presence—sometimes so much so, that we are as astonished as Peter was by the 153 large fish.

Fourth Sunday of Easter

The Gospel of John 10:27–30

[Jesus said,] "My sheep hear my voice, and I know them, and they follow me; and I give them eternal life, and they shall never perish, and no one shall snatch them out of my hand. My Father, who has given them to me, is greater than all, and no one is able to snatch them out of the Father's hand. I and the Father are one."

They Know His Voice

This fourth Sunday in the season of Easter is called "Good Shepherd Sunday". Various passages from Jesus' "shepherd discourse" are read—today quite a short one, but full of significance. "I am the good shepherd. The good shepherd lays down his life for the sheep" is what Jesus had said just before (Jn 10:11). He had warned his hearers against the false shepherds, the hirelings who are thinking only of their own profit and are indifferent to the welfare of the flock.

How can the flock know who is the good shepherd and who is the bad one? Jesus, as he so often does, refers to everyday experience. He reminds his audience of what they all know from the shepherds' way of life, with which people were familiar in those days. "When he [the shepherd] has brought out [from the fold] all his own [sheep], he goes before them, and the sheep follow him, for they know his voice. A stranger they will not follow, but they will flee from him, for they do not know the voice of strangers" (Jn 10:4–5).

So it is by his voice that they know him. The sound of the shepherd's voice is the sign for the sheep that they can trust him. He knows them, and they know him. What was Jesus trying to say through this parable? The first and most important thing is that he knows his sheep. He knows me better than I know myself. How much do I know about myself? Other people often know me better and see my weaknesses and strengths more clearly than I do myself. Yet even if I make great strides in self-knowledge, I still remain a riddle to myself.

He knows me, not just a little bit, but through and through. God alone knows what is really in a man's heart. It says in the Catechism, "God is omniscient." But that is not something to strike fear in us. He is not "Big Brother", the great watcher who sees all, spying into men's ultimate intimacies, the one from whom I cannot keep the least little corner hidden.

He knows me as the shepherd knows his sheep. He knows what we need, and he means to lead his flock to good pastures. "I give you eternal life", says Jesus, the Good Shepherd. He does not know us in order to condemn us but in order to lead us safely to the pastures of eternal life. Just as the Good Shepherd fights for the life of his sheep and protects them from predators, so Jesus declares energetically, "They shall never perish, and no one shall snatch them out of my hand."

Have no fear of God's omniscience! It is inseparable from his mercy. It is comforting to know that nothing is hidden from him, for he does not condemn us. And yet there are so many voices that condemn me! We are continually criticizing one another, and we are always finding fault with the other person—there is always a fly in his ointment. And then there is always that other voice in my heart, accusing me: "You ought to have done that differently!" Self-criticism and self-reproaches—sometimes, unfortunately, well founded, whenever we have really made mistakes. A buzz of voices that often threatens to drive us mad.

Yet here is a voice that sounds different. "My sheep hear my voice." It does you good, it does not condemn you—nor does it butter you up. This voice tells me the truth, yet it is full of love and kindness. It is his voice, the voice of the Good Shepherd.

It can speak to me in my heart, through the Bible, or through people I love. Distinguishing its tones among all the other noise is of vital importance. For he whose voice this is, is leading me along a good path. I can trust this voice completely. It is leading me along the path to life.

Fifth Sunday of Easter

The Gospel of John 13:31–33a, 34–35

When [Judas] had gone out, Jesus said, "Now is the Son of man glorified, and in him is God glorified; if God is glorified in him, God will also glorify him in himself, and glorify him at once. Little children, yet a little while I am with you. . . . A new commandment I give to you, that you love one another; even as I have loved you, that you also love one another. By this all men will know that you are my disciples, if you have love for one another."

What Was Important to Jesus

Up to Pentecost, for three weeks, the Church reads extracts from Jesus' so-called farewell discourses. At the Last Supper, on the night before he died, Jesus talked for a long time to his friends, his disciples, making things explicit. Now and then, they interrupted him with a question. And they had quite a few questions: "What is happening to you?" "Why do you have to suffer?" "Where are you going when you die?" "What will happen to us when you have gone away?" "Will we see each other again?"

We can sense, in what Jesus says and in the questions his Apostles ask, all the sorrow and difficulty of saying good-bye: "Yet a little while I am with you; soon you will no longer see me." Yet confidence can be felt even more strongly. "I will not leave you desolate" [Jn 14:18], he says in the course of the evening, to those whom he lovingly calls his "little children". And he does what fathers and mothers do whenever they are able to take proper leave of their children before dying: they entrust them with whatever was most important to them in life. And they give them advice, advice that they are never to forget, for making their way in life.

It is with that kind of fatherly or motherly concern that Jesus speaks to those who belong to him. And his words hold good not just for that occasion. They have lasting validity for all those who are trying to be his disciples. That is why Jesus' farewell discourses are also known as his "testament".

We find two sayings that show us the way in today's Gospel reading. The first concerns Jesus himself. Judas has just left them; he has gone out into the night to betray Jesus. Very soon he will be leading the little troop of men who are to take Jesus captive. He will show them the way to where they can find Jesus, among the innumerable Passover pilgrims.

At that dramatic moment, Jesus says, "Now God is glorifying me, and I him." For the moment, those with him at table can hardly grasp what that is supposed to mean. Later it became clear to them. What looked like helplessness was in reality the beginning of something glorious. He was delivered helpless into the hands of his enemies. He goes along with this—yet not against his will but quite readily, because he certainly believes and knows that his way of the Cross, which is beginning right then, is not meaningless. He intends to do God's will, and God's will leads to what is good, however much the situation seems, from a human point of view, utterly desperate.

Jesus teaches us to trust "that in everything God works for good with those who love him" (Rom 8:28), as Paul puts it. Everything, even the most difficult situations, leads to something good, if we trust in God. The way of Jesus shows us something else as well, of course: God does not spare him the Cross. It often takes a long time before the good things that are being given through the Cross become apparent. Jesus' bequest to us is that we can trust in him, as he trusted in God his Father.

And he mentions a second bequest. This is his great request: "Children, love one another!" How often that is the concern of parents when they are dying, that the children should be tolerant of each other. Jesus wants more than that: they are to love one another just as much as he has loved them. Nothing is more wretched than when his children, who call themselves Christians, proffer each other hatred and strife instead of love. That clouds many other people's view of Jesus. That is why, at the hour when he is saying good-bye, Jesus is most keenly concerned that his disciples should genuinely, simply and honestly love one another. "By this all men will know that you are my disciples." We still have quite a bit to do to fulfill the last will of Jesus!

Sixth Sunday of Easter

The Gospel of John 14:23–29

Jesus answered him, "If a man loves me, he will keep my word, and my Father will love him, and we will come to him and make our home with him. He who does not love me does not keep my words; and the word which you hear is not mine but the Father's who sent me.

"These things I have spoken to you, while I am still with you. But the Counselor, the Holy Spirit, whom the Father will send in my name, he will teach you all things, and bring to your remembrance all that I have said to you. Peace I leave with you; my peace I give to you; not as the world gives do I give to you. Let not your hearts be troubled, neither let them be afraid. You heard me say to you, 'I go away, and I will come to you.' If you loved me, you would have rejoiced, because I go to the Father; for the Father is greater than I. And now I have told you before it takes place, so that when it does take place, you may believe."

Where God Dwells

Words of farewell. On this Sixth Sunday in Easter, too, the Gospel reading is taken from the farewell discourses of Jesus. In the hours of the night before he was taken captive, Jesus talked at length to his friends. He confided to them what was most important to him—his testament, so to speak. Every word here is weighty. It is all so dense with significance that we need a great deal of time to grasp the meaning of his words. People have been meditating on them, and drawing strength from them, for almost two thousand years.

One saying here has always struck people's notice: "We will come to him and make our home with him." How can God "make his home" with a human being, as it says literally? The Christian mystics have often talked about this saying. Teachers of the spiritual life see in this one of Jesus' most marvelous promises. What does it mean?

God does not live in heaven alone, in that world of his "up above", far away from earth. He also dwells in our midst, and even more so, within us. God is the one who is entirely other-worldly and entirely indwelling. The sense that God is present in all things—in stones and in plants, in animals and in people—is alive in many religions. To specify that, faith says that God is omnipresent. Yet his presence is not of equal strength everywhere. In nature, whether animate or inanimate, God is there as its Creator, with his power that creates and upholds everything, his power that holds the atoms together and gives growth to the flowers and life to the animals.

God desires to be even more powerfully present in us men: he desires to make his home with us, like a neighbor, a friend, or a beloved: "If a man loves me, he will keep my word, and my Father will love him, and we will come to him and make our home with him."

How can we tell that God has made his dwelling with us? We can see and hear our neighbor, regardless of whether this irritates us or rejoices us. We can talk to a fellow resident of our house. We can embrace our beloved. But God?

Jesus says that he will come with the Father and with the Holy Spirit. Can we be aware of this coming? How, and in what ways? Many people really do have the experience of

God coming into their lives. I am thinking of the Franciscan writer André Frossard (d. 1995), who described his conversion ("God does exist. I have met him") in a widely read book. God suddenly came into his life and changed it from top to bottom. Mostly, however, God's coming is a gentle, step-by-step affair, as if he wanted to allow us to get used to his presence gradually, without alarming us.

Jesus says that is what the Holy Spirit, whom he calls the "advocate" or "counselor", effects in us: He will "bring to your remembrance all that I have said to you". Listening to the "inner voice", to what our heart and our conscience say to us, brings God close. Listening to what Jesus says and keeping to it, keeping hold of it, brings about his dwelling with us. God is everywhere, and everything is filled with his presence. But he desires to "make his home" with us, as a bosom friend.

The Ascension of Our Lord

The Gospel of Luke 24:46–53

[Then he] said to them, "Thus it is written, that the Christ should suffer and on the third day rise from the dead, and that repentance and forgiveness of sins should be preached in his name to all nations, beginning from Jerusalem. You are witnesses of these things. And behold, I send the promise of my Father upon you; but stay in the city, until you are clothed with power from on high."

Then he led them out as far as Bethany, and lifting up his hands he blessed them. While he blessed them, he parted from them and was carried up into heaven. And they worshiped him, and returned to Jerusalem with great joy, and were continually in the temple blessing God.

An Ascension—to Where?

The Ascension of our Lord—one of those Thursday holidays that make difficulties for the economy and that many people would like to do away with, as has already happened in other countries. Why should we celebrate this day—what is, in fact, its original meaning? Is not the picture of Jesus' Ascension a concept that is long obsolete in the space age? Do we have any use at all for the idea of a heaven in which Jesus Christ is sitting "at the right hand of God" [Mk 16:19]? The whole point of this feast seems to be fading from view. And yet a holiday for the Ascension will survive in the long run only if its religious meaning remains a living thing. How can this meaning be understood in a new way for today?

First, a word on the subject of heaven. Luke reports that "while he blessed them, he parted from them and was carried up into heaven." The heaven being talked about here is not outer space. Where could there be a place, in the inconceivable vastness of the universe, that we could call "heaven"? The Ascension of our Lord is not a journey into space. Jesus said, in another place, what it means: "I go to the Father." Ascension is going home. It is not to his earthly home that Jesus is returning; his Resurrection was not a return to earthly life. Rather, he went back to the place from whence he had come: into the world of God. That is also the true home of man. It is the goal of the pilgrimage, often arduous and laborious, of life in this world.

What does God's heaven look like? We do not know; we can form only the vaguest notion of it and believe that God has, as Jesus once said, "prepared a dwelling for us" there [see Jn 14:2–3]. A man's way through life has been well accomplished, not if he has been successful, become famous, or made a lot of money, but only if he has not failed to reach his eternal goal.

Jesus himself is at the same time signpost and path to this goal. That is what his Ascension shows. First Jesus had to suffer. His disciples found it hard to cope with this at the time, and they still do. Why did the suffering happen? What was the Cross for? That is the way that leads to conversion. We are purified through the suffering. No one can find a way to "slip in to" heaven, without reflection and repentance, without changing his life and his heart. That is why Jesus talked very seriously about the restricted entrance, the narrow path, that leads to eternal life. He even used the image of the eye of a needle. It is obviously not so simple to find one's way home through all life's wrong turns.

Yet Jesus knows what great dangers we run. He knows our weaknesses as no one else does. That is why he came, why he became man, as our brother and our Master, so as not only to show us the way but to go before us, on our behalf, upon it. He took on himself all the weight of our failures and overcame it. His Ascension is our way home. "He did not hide himself behind the clouds", says Saint Augustine, but "he has installed heaven in the hearts of his friends". We no longer see him, but "he is beginning to breathe in us".

Perhaps that is why, after his Ascension, his disciples are so filled with joy. They now know at what they are aiming, and they know that Jesus will be their constant and invisible companion on their journey. With him, we will surely reach home.

Seventh Sunday of Easter

The Gospel of John 17:20–26

[Jesus lifted up his eyes to heaven and said, "Father,] I do not pray for these only, but also for those who believe in me through their word, that they may all be one; even as you, Father, are in me, and I in you, that they also may be in us, so that the world may believe that you have sent me. The glory which you have given me I have given to them, that they may be one even as we are one, I in them and you in me, that they may become perfectly one, so that the world may know that you have sent me and have loved them even as you have loved me. Father, I desire that they also, whom you have given me, may be with me where I am, to behold my glory which you have given me in your love for me before the foundation of the world. O righteous Father, the world has not known you, but I have known you; and these know that you have sent me. I made known to them your name, and I will make it known, that the love with which you have loved me may be in them, and I in them."

They Are to Be One

What will happen next? What will happen after I have gone? This is a question, a concern, that much occupies a father or a mother when it is time to take leave of this life, when death draws near. In those last hours, anyone who is able to believe will entrust these concerns to God and will leave them in his hands.

Jesus did something like that on the night before his suffering and death. Together with his little troop of faithful followers (who will, of course, almost all leave him in the lurch very soon), he is there for a meal in the upper room of an ordinary house in Jerusalem. It is a serious moment, full of worries. The religious authorities are looking for him; they have decided to have him killed. They are afraid that he will win the people over to his side, so that it could result in disturbances, in uprisings against the Romans, and that would result in still more oppression and lack of freedom for the Jewish people. And that is why the highest religious leader of the people, the high priest Caiaphas, has said, "It is expedient for you that one man should die for the people, and that the whole nation should not perish" [Jn 11:50]. He had no idea how true this saying was. Jesus really did die for the whole Jewish people—indeed, for all people—in order to reconcile them to God. That is how Jesus himself understood the meaning of his death: that is what he lived for, and that is what he died for. And, so we believe, he is still living for that even now, because he did not remain among the dead but rose again.

The way that Jesus was not primarily concerned for himself but for others finds expression in the long prayer from which today's Gospel reading is taken. This is the longest of Jesus' prayers that has been transmitted to us, with his principal requests to God his Father. In these requests we may see what was closest to Jesus' heart. He prayed first for his disciples, to whom he was saying good-bye. He entrusted them with the whole of his appointed task. They were to carry it on. They were to take his message out. And so Jesus prayed not merely for his Apostles but for those who were going to "believe in me through their word".

What is on my mind at this point is the idea that, in this final hour, Jesus prayed for all those multitudes who would, at some point in the coming centuries, believe in him. He prayed for me, too, and for all those people to whom I am indebted for being able to believe. He also prayed for all those to whom I try to pass on his message. They were, all of them, already in his heart then.

And what did he ask of God his Father in that decisive hour? In first place comes his great request, "that they all may be one". When parents are at the hour of their death, it is often their heaviest care when there are divisions between the children. That is what Jesus most urgently implores, that those who belong to him may be one. Did Jesus know, in that hour, how disunited his future believers would often be? Certainly, since it was in fact for that reason that he died, that they should be one; and only when they look to him and hold fast to him will they be able to manage to be at one among themselves. They are to love one another, as Jesus is at one with his Father in love. It is good to know that Jesus himself is praying that that should come about. And often, it really does.

Pentecost Sunday

The Gospel of John 20:19–23

On the evening of that day, the first day of the week, the doors being shut where the disciples were, for fear of the Jews, Jesus came and stood among them and said to them, "Peace be with you." When he had said this, he showed them his hands and his side. Then the disciples were glad when they saw the Lord. Jesus said to them again, "Peace be with you. As the Father has sent me, even so I send you." And when he had said this, he breathed on them, and said to them, "Receive the Holy Spirit. If you forgive the sins of any, they are forgiven; if you retain the sins of any, they are retained."

A New Pentecost

The word "Pentecost" comes from the Greek and means simply "fiftieth". We celebrate many "fiftieths": birthdays, memorials, and jubilees.

Pentecost is simply the fiftieth day after Easter, the golden Easter Day, so to speak. That is why the Gospel reading from Easter Day is read again today. Easter is indeed not in the past. Christ is risen. Death no longer has any power over him. That is why he was able to promise that he will remain with us every day until the end of the world. And that is why he has pledged that his Church will never ever be overpowered by death or by the forces of destruction.

Time and again there has been "a new Pentecost", which has reawakened and renewed the Church. Blessed Pope John XXIII was hoping for just such a new Pentecost, when he called a council* nearly fifty years ago to renew the Church. Did it happen? Did it fail to come about? How can we know, how can we judge, whether the Holy Spirit is bringing about a new Pentecost?

The Gospel reading shows us how. The starting point is an unpleasant and hopeless situation, one that offers no comfort. Jesus' disciples are sitting together helplessly, with no idea what to do. Fear holds them in its bonds. The doors are barred from the inside, and probably the windows, too. Their talking and thinking turns around their own difficulties; they are bewailing the hard times and the wicked world. Former times, when things were better, are nostalgically evoked. The view ahead strikes fear into them, and looking back becomes a way of escaping present difficulties.

Who has not known times like that? We have them in our personal lives, just as in the life of the Church. These are moments of profound depression. No light appears; we see no end to the tunnel.

Then Jesus comes, right in among the disciples. Barred doors and windows are no obstacle to him. What happened on the evening of Easter Day has gone on happening, up to this day, with ever-new and surprising twists. What seemed dead comes to life; what seemed to be dead-end situations becomes the new way forward. I call that "the turning point of hope". I believe we can recognize a new Pentecost from the way hope burgeons afresh.

We have a great longing for such a turning point: finally emerging from the diabolical circle of addiction; finding

* Vatican Council II (1962–1965).

peace in the endless conflict of a difficult relationship; being set free from the tormenting sense of meaninglessness and uselessness. We can continue the list as long as we like. Yet how does the turnaround come about? Back then, it was Christ himself who came, visibly and tangibly, and brought peace and joy. But what about today?

There are many ways in which Christ gives us new hope. It mostly happens through other people, who light up our darkness. For many people, Pope John XXIII brought a glimmer of hope. Many found the same thing with Cardinal Franz König (d. 2004). Often it is quite ordinary people through whom the joy of Christ comes into our lives. Such encounters can change people's lives.

What is quite decisive, however, is that we encounter God's mercy. "If you forgive the sins of any . . ." says Jesus, on the evening of Easter Day. Without forgiveness, there is no hope. We can see that, in the dreadful trouble spots of today's world. We have all the more need of people who are prepared to pass on to others the peace and reconciliation of Jesus, so that a new Pentecost may come.

Feasts

in the

Church Year

Trinity Sunday

The Gospel of John 16:12–15

[Jesus said to his disciples,] "I have yet many things to say to you, but you cannot bear them now. When the Spirit of truth comes, he will guide you into all the truth; for he will not speak on his own authority, but whatever he hears he will speak, and he will declare to you the things that are to come. He will glorify me, for he will take what is mine and declare it to you. All that the Father has is mine; therefore I said that he will take what is mine and declare it to you."

A Mission to Shake the World

It is a question that affects the whole world, religious and political, one decisive for the future: Did Jesus say it all, or is there something important still to come? Was Jesus the ultimate and decisive messenger from God, or is this messenger still to come? Was Jesus' message just one stage, or was it the climax and conclusion of what God has to say to the world?

"Typical theological hair splitting", you may say. "These questions may occupy the minds of scholars but not the hearts of ordinary people." These questions, which many people have failed to consider, are decisive for a great part of what is happening in the world today. The greatest religious community on earth, Christianity, is persuaded that Jesus Christ is the Son of God and that in him God has said everything essential to the world and has done all that is essential for us men. The second greatest religion, Islam, sees in Jesus a prophet, an important messenger from God, but, for Islam, the ultimately valid revelation did not come through Jesus, but through the Quran, which Muhammad received from God.

And someone might still say, "Well, they ought to argue it out between them as to who is right! But what has that got to do with my life?" Nowadays, the discord affects pretty nearly the whole world. For each of the two religions bases its claim on the mission given by its founder and is busy trying to win all men to their beliefs. Both of them are missionary religions, working worldwide to spread their faith. A mission to the whole world is part of both Christianity and Islam and is part of their practice. Their methods, in doing so, have not always been peaceful—nor are they, still. Often, unfortunately, compulsion and force have played a part—and still do today. That certainly does not correspond to the mission Jesus gave us. He certainly did not assign anyone the task of making people believe in him and in his message. His intention was to win people's hearts through what he said, by his example and above all by giving up his life, and to present them with God's merciful love. And he entrusted his faithful with the task of leading people to belief in exactly that way—and only in that way.

But what does all that have to do with today's Gospel reading? It raises precisely this question: Has Jesus already said all there is? "I have yet many things to say to you, but you cannot bear them now." During his earthly lifetime, did Jesus hold back on many things, which were going to be revealed only later? Then it might really be true that only later prophets have completed what Jesus began. In that case, Jesus might really have been only a stage in the process.

Jesus himself, so we believe, saw things differently. Just before this [today's reading], he said to his disciples in the room where they held the Last Supper, "I have called you friends, for all that I have heard from my Father I have made known to you" (Jn 15:15). Jesus really did bring the whole of God's message. He is the "beloved Son", in whose person God has made his greatest gift to the world. Only we are too small to be able to grasp it in its entirety straightaway. Our hearts are not yet large enough to accept the whole of this gift.

That is why Jesus promised that he would send us his Spirit, to lead us, step by step, deeper and deeper into the truth. Bit by bit, the Holy Spirit makes our hearts bigger and more spacious, so that we may gradually perceive what Jesus means for us. God's method in doing this is not by using force but by patiently guiding and leading us on. One day, perhaps not until the Last Day, we shall see how very much God truly loves us.

Corpus Christi

The Gospel of Luke 9:11b–17

[Jesus welcomed the crowds] and spoke to them of the kingdom of God, and cured those who had need of healing. Now the day began to wear away; and the Twelve came and said to him, "Send the crowd away, to go into the villages and country round about, to lodge and get provisions; for we are here in a lonely place." But he said to them, "You give them something to eat." They said, "We have no more than five loaves and two fish—unless we are to go and buy food for all these people." For there were about five thousand men. And he said to his disciples, "Make them sit down in companies, about fifty each." And they did so, and made them all sit down. And taking the five loaves and the two fish he looked up to heaven, and blessed and broke them, and gave them to the disciples to set before the crowd. And all ate and were satisfied. And they took up what was left over, twelve baskets of broken pieces.

Give Them Something to Eat

Mother Teresa (d. 1997) once received as a gift an extremely valuable jewel, a great ruby. To universal surprise, she directed that this should be set on the tabernacle of the sisters' chapel in Calcutta. People objected that it would make more sense to sell the stone for a great sum of money, so as to be able to help the poor. She is supposed to have said, "When Christ is no longer revered, then people will soon pay no more attention to the poor."

She desired that the tabernacle, in which the sacred Host, the Eucharistic Bread, the Body of Christ, was reserved, should be especially honored. At Corpus Christi, the sacred Host is given reverence in quite extraordinary and solemn fashion. Everywhere, there are processions, and the priest carries the monstrance—which is usually of precious metal. He carries Jesus, in the form of bread, through the streets and into the public squares. People keen to see the show line the path of the procession. Many furtively make the sign of the Cross, or even genuflect, when the "heaven" canopy is carried past, with the precious monstrance and the sacred Host beneath it.

Does that still make sense today? Many critics of the Corpus Christi processions say that Jesus did not command us to carry his Body around but said, "Take, eat" [Mt 26:26]. And today's Gospel reading in particular shows that Jesus was concerned for people in need—those lacking bread, those who go hungry: "Give them something to eat" is what he demands of his disciples.

With only five loaves and two fishes, Jesus satisfied the hunger of around five thousand people—and he did this so completely that there were twelve baskets full of food left over. Miracles like this have been repeated time after time in the long history of the Church. Some of them are historically well attested.

The miracle of the feeding of the five thousand served first, and above all, to help people in need. It was, however, also something like a foreshadowing, an anticipation, of that still-greater miracle that right up to this day occurs daily, throughout the world, wherever the Holy Mass is celebrated!

The feast of Corpus Christi is intended to honor this greater mystery. That is why, everywhere, the bread that has become the Body of Christ is carried in solemn procession. Once more: Does that make sense in view of the great want there is in the world? Is it not more important to see to people's bodily needs and to fight against hunger in the world?

I am thinking now of the saying of Mother Teresa, who was mentioned at the beginning. She never forgot to revere Christ in the sacred Host, in the Blessed Sacrament, just as we do at Corpus Christi. For it was from him that she heard and accepted the command, "Do not send people away! Give them something to eat!" The Missionaries of Charity, in the Order she founded, are doing that among the poorest people, all over the world. They draw strength to do this, day by day, from Christ in the tabernacle.

The Immaculate Conception of Mary

The Gospel of Luke 1:26–38

In the sixth month the angel Gabriel was sent from God to a city of Galilee named Nazareth, to a virgin betrothed to a man whose name was Joseph, of the house of David; and the virgin's name was Mary. And he came to her and said, "Hail, full of grace, the Lord is with you!" But she was greatly troubled at the saying, and considered in her mind what sort of greeting this might be. And the angel said to her, "Do not be afraid, Mary, for you have found favor with God. And behold, you will conceive in your womb and bear a son, and you shall call his name Jesus.

He will be great, and will be called the Son of the
Most High;
and the Lord God will give to him the throne of his
father David,
and he will reign over the house of Jacob
for ever;
and of his kingdom there will be no end."

And Mary said to the angel, "How can this be, since I have no husband?" And the angel said to her,

"The Holy Spirit will come upon you,
and the power of the Most High will
overshadow you;
therefore the child to be born will be called holy,
the Son of God.

And behold, your kinswoman Elizabeth in her old age has also conceived a son; and this is the sixth month with her who was called barren. For with God nothing will be impossible." And Mary said, "Behold, I am the handmaid of the Lord; let it be to me according to your word." And the angel departed from her.

Take a Breather instead of Shopping

On December 8, 1854, Pope Pius IX (d. 1878) promulgated the dogma of the Immaculate Conception of Mary. What motivated him to take that step? Certainly not any momentary whim. Mary, the Mother of Jesus, had already been honored for centuries as the one who was "conceived without the stain of original sin". In churches and chapels, we may see countless representations of Mary as the "Immaculata". Many statues in public places bear witness to how Mary was greatly revered as the person of "immaculate conception". The old bronze pillar of Mary "am Hof" in Vienna is particularly beautiful; it is a commemoration of a great danger in time of war, when in 1647 the Swedes threatened Vienna, and the emperor entrusted our country to the special protection of the Mother of God.

Until fifty years ago, there was great enthusiasm for this dogma in Austria. At that time, there rose a great wave of prayer and of expressions of people's political will. In the year in which Austria was liberated, there was a quite unique petition for the reinstatement of December 8 as a public holiday, which had been abolished by Hitler. It was the biggest plebiscite of the Second Republic! The consequence was that December 8 once more became a holiday.

It has theoretically remained so up to this day. In practice, however, it has long since been sacrificed to the "god" called "Christmas shopping". I can understand that a little. For when the meaning of some festival begins to fade from people's mentality, then it will inevitably be abolished. Then all the protests of bishops and lay people just die away in the face of economics and politics. Business must go on.

What has faded may become glowing and fresh once more. For many of our ancestors, this was a radiantly beautiful and beloved mystery of the faith. Why should it not become so again today? It concerns Mary and her conception nine months before her birth (December 8 to September 8).

All there is to be said about the feast of her conception can be summed up in one saying, which is at the heart of today's Gospel reading about the Annunciation of the conception of Jesus within Mary: "Hail, full of grace, the Lord is with you!"

There are many people who are endowed with grace. Each person has natural gifts, talents, and endowments. Above and beyond that, special graces are attributed to each person by God, graces of faith, of perseverance, of kindness, and many more. Yet none of us can say that we are "full of grace". We all of us carry within us stains and failings, dark and unpurified elements.

Mary did not become "full of grace" but was so from the beginning; from the first moment of her existence, she was immaculate. God created her wholly and entirely clear and filled with light, without any stain. If in our times, which are brimming with filth, the longing for purity should once more become greater, then we shall experience a new joy in celebrating December 8 and will "take a breather" instead of shopping. The loveliest Christmas present is, in fact, Mary with her babe. It is worth thanking God for that in particular, especially on the feast today.

The Assumption of the Blessed Virgin Mary

The Gospel of Luke 1:39–56

In those days Mary arose and went with haste into the hill country, to a city of Judah, and she entered the house of Zechariah and greeted Elizabeth. And when Elizabeth heard the greeting of Mary, the child leaped in her womb; and Elizabeth was filled with the Holy Spirit and she exclaimed with a loud cry, "Blessed are you among women, and blessed is the fruit of your womb! And why is this granted me, that the mother of my Lord should come to me? For behold, when the voice of your greeting came to my ears, the child in my womb leaped for joy. And blessed is she who believed that there would be a fulfilment of what was spoken to her from the Lord." And Mary said,

"My soul magnifies the Lord,
and my spirit rejoices in God my Savior,
for he has regarded the low estate of his handmaiden.
For behold, henceforth all generations will call me blessed;
for he who is mighty has done great things for me,
and holy is his name.
And his mercy is on those who fear him
from generation to generation.
He has shown strength with his arm,
he has scattered the proud in the imagination of their hearts,
he has put down the mighty from their thrones,
and exalted those of low degree;

he has filled the hungry with good things,
and the rich he has sent empty away.
He has helped his servant Israel,
in remembrance of his mercy,
as he spoke to our fathers,
to Abraham and to his posterity for ever."

And Mary remained with her about three months, and returned to her home.

A Blessed Body

Ordinary people in Austria still call today's feast simply "the Ascension of Mary", even though the official ecclesiastical and liturgical title is "the Solemnity of the Assumption of the Blessed Virgin Mary into Heaven". "Lammas", as it is also traditionally known, is still so popular, even in the Europe of today, that it remains an official public holiday in many countries. I know of no instance of economists or politicians seriously calling this holiday into question so far, nor of their calling for its abolition.

There is no doubt that "the Ascension of Mary", the Assumption, is one of the best-loved Marian feasts. Yet what is the situation concerning the significance and the importance of the content of this feast? What does "bodily assumption into heaven" mean? How about the biblical basis of this event? Is it not strange that the Bible tells us nothing about it? The Gospel reading for this feast is talking about a quite different occurrence: the visit of the young, pregnant Mary to her relative Elizabeth, who is expecting a baby despite her age and is in the sixth month of her pregnancy.

There are only legendary accounts of the earthly life of

Mary, nothing historically reliable. Mary is supposed to have "fallen asleep", passed away (the Christian East calls this feast "the Dormition of Mary", to this day), but the tomb was afterward found empty by the Apostles. The nugget of truth at the heart of the legend, however, is to be found in today's Gospel reading. This has to do with pregnancy and life. Two women, Mary and Elizabeth, meet. Each is carrying a baby under her heart. When they greet each other and embrace, the babies move in their wombs as if they, too, meant to greet each other.

The mystery of life! No living man has ever come into the world except by being born of a woman, his mother. In spite of all the wars, all the violence and destruction, all the power of death, this mystery of life is still stronger. That is what the faithful felt from an early stage: the body that gave life to Jesus could not simply fall victim to death.

Elizabeth was perhaps the first to have an inkling of it, when she welcomed Mary, her young relative, with the unusual greeting "Blessed are you among women, and blessed is the fruit of your womb!" Since then, people at prayer have reiterated this greeting countless times, whenever they pray the Hail Mary. Mary herself, in the "hymn of thanksgiving" with which she responded to Elizabeth's greeting, said, "Behold, henceforth all generations will call me blessed." And all generations since then have in fact expressed their love and gratitude toward Mary. There is no nation upon earth today among which she is not honored. She is no goddess—she is fully and entirely human—but she is blessed like no other human being. For she is, as Elizabeth says in her greeting, "the mother of my Lord". She gave him earthly life, and he gave her heavenly life, for body and soul. Because she is already living with him fully, she is, constantly, fully with other people.

All Saints

The Gospel of Matthew 5:1–12a

Seeing the crowds, [Jesus] went up on the mountain, and when he sat down his disciples came to him. And he opened his mouth and taught them, saying:

"Blessed are the poor in spirit, for theirs is the kingdom of heaven.

"Blessed are those who mourn, for they shall be comforted.

"Blessed are the meek, for they shall inherit the earth.

"Blessed are those who hunger and thirst for righteousness, for they shall be satisfied.

"Blessed are the merciful, for they shall obtain mercy.

"Blessed are the pure in heart, for they shall see God.

"Blessed are the peacemakers, for they shall be called sons of God.

"Blessed are those who are persecuted for righteousness' sake, for theirs is the kingdom of heaven.

"Blessed are you when men revile you and persecute you and utter all kinds of evil against you falsely on my account. Rejoice and be glad, for your reward is great in heaven, for so men persecuted the prophets who were before you."

The Countless Host

In the old archepiscopal library in Vienna there stands an impressive row of perhaps thirty folio volumes, books in large format with thick wooden endboards finished in leather. This work is called *Acta Sanctorum*, the lives and works of the saints. For each day of the year, the acts, documents, and descriptions of the lives of saints of every century have been collected by zealous researchers of the seventeenth and eighteenth centuries and have been set down in chronological order.

It is incredible, the materials that have been brought together there. What is most impressive of all, however, is the enormous host of saints. Each day there are thirty, forty, or more saints' names, with their stories.

If, occasionally, I am reading something in these heavy tomes early in the morning or late at night (everything is in Latin), then I have to think of the seer of Patmos, of the Revelation of Saint John, also known as the "Apocalypse". In his prophetic vision, he sees "up above" in heaven "a great multitude which no man could number, from every nation, from all tribes and peoples and tongues" (Rev 7:9).

Truly, no one can count the number of saints. Besides the thousands who are inscribed in the *Acta Sanctorum*, there are the many saints who have been added since then—that is, in the past two hundred years. Pope John Paul II (d. 2005) alone undertook the declaration of 1,338 people as "blessed", and of 482 as saints. He did not "invent" them, nor did he "make" them saints. He merely made known what was already the case: that these were fascinating people who lived out the gospel fully, Christians who took seriously what Jesus proclaims in today's Gospel reading.

Eight times, Jesus says, "Blessed are the . . ." or "Blessed are those . . ." Eight times, he tells us what is needed for someone to make a success of life. For saints are not some kind of separate species but are people whose lives have achieved their goal, people who have walked along the road of happiness.

It is a great sign of hope that there are so many of them who were merciful instead of being hardhearted; who brought peace where hatred and strife had reigned; who demanded righteousness instead of going along with injustice; who preferred to accept being persecuted for the sake of righteousness rather than run with the pack; who were prepared to endure disgrace rather than denigrate other people.

People like that are upright at heart, pure in heart. They do you good; it is good to be with them. They are not among those people who build themselves up at the expense of others. They would rather console others than seek consolation themselves; they are not the center of their own lives, and that is why their hands and their hearts are free for other people. They are not full of their own importance, but, like a bowl that is standing empty and uncovered, they are ready for God to pour his love into them, that it may overflow for others.

That is who the saints are. It is encouraging to see that they are not so rare, that they are not exceptional cases. They are, indeed, a countless multitude. For those whose names are inscribed in the massive folios of the archepiscopal library are only a tiny fraction of those who are saints before God—even though, on earth, hardly anybody knows anything about them. Today the Church thinks with gratitude and confidence of all those many people, a countless host, who are still doing good on earth today—and, indeed, today more than ever before. Even more than in their earthly lifetimes.

Index

FOR THE THREE VOLUMES OF COMMENTARIES
ON THE GOSPEL READINGS

A *My Jesus*
B *Behold, God's Son*
C *Jesus, the Divine Physician*

GOSPEL OF MARK

GOSPEL OF LUKE

GOSPEL OF JOHN